IRAN
in Pictures

Stacy Taus-Bolstad

Lerner Publications Company

Contents

Lerner Publishing Group realizes that current information and statistics quickly become out of date. To extend the usefulness of the Visual Geography Series, we developed www.vgsbooks.com, a website offering links to up-to-date information, as well as in-depth material, on a wide variety of subjects. All of the websites listed on www.vgsbooks.com have been carefully selected by researchers at Lerner Publishing Group. However, Lerner Publishing Group is not responsible for the accuracy or suitability of the material on any website other than <www.lernerbooks.com>. It is recommended that students using the Internet be supervised by a parent or teacher. Links on www.vgsbooks.com will be regularly reviewed and updated as needed.

INTRODUCTION   4

THE LAND   8

▶ Topography. Bodies of Water. Climate. Flora and
Fauna. Environmental Issues. Cities.

HISTORY AND GOVERNMENT   20

▶ The Persians. Foreign Rulers. The Safavid Shahs.
Outside Influence. Reza Shah and World War II.
Mohammed Reza Pahlavi. Becoming an Islamic
Republic. Conflict with Iraq. Problems and
Reforms. Government.

THE PEOPLE   36

▶ Ethnic Groups. Religion. Social Customs and the
Role of Women. Education. Health.

CURR
QS
254 T
J3kg
2004

Website address: www.lernerbooks.com

Lerner Publications Company
A division of Lerner Publishing Group
241 First Avenue North
Minneapolis, MN 55401 U.S.A.

web enhanced @ www.vgsbooks.com

CULTURAL LIFE   46

► Language and Literature. Arts and Crafts.
  Architecture. Theater and Film. Music. Holidays and
  Festivals. Food and Clothing. Sports and Recreation.

THE ECONOMY   56

► Oil and Mining. Industry. Agriculture and Fishing.
  Heroin and Opium. Transportation and
  Communication. The Future.

FOR MORE INFORMATION

► Timeline   66
► Fast Facts   68
► Currency   68
► Flag   69
► National Anthem   69
► Famous People   70
► Sights to See   72
► Glossary   73
► Selected Bibliography   74
► Further Reading and Websites   76
► Index   78

Library of Congress Cataloging-in-Publication Data

Taus-Bolstad, Stacy.
        Iran in pictures / by Stacy Taus-Bolstad.—Rev. & expanded.
           p.   cm. — (Visual geography series)
        Summary: Text and illustrations present detailed information on the geography, history and
government, economy, people, cultural life, and society of traditional and modern Iran.
        Includes bibliographical references and index.
        ISBN: 0-8225-0950-4 (lib. bdg. : alk. paper)
        1. Iran—Juvenile literature. 2. Iran—Pictorial works—Juvenile literature. [1. Iran.] I. Title. II. Visual
geography series (Minneapolis, Minn.)
DS254.75.T384 2004
953.8—dc21   2001002967

Manufactured in the United States of America
1 2 3 4 5 6 - JR - 09 08 07 06 05 04

INTRODUCTION

Iran is a nation of contrasts. Located in the Middle East, the land features soaring mountains and low valleys, barren deserts and lush coastal lands. Iran's weather is marked by freezing winters and scorching summers. The country's political system faces serious international and internal challenges, but it remains one of the strongest governments in the Middle East. The nation is rich in oil resources, yet its economy remains largely underdeveloped.

Ancient history has also helped to shape Iran. Long referred to as Persia, Iran did not officially become the name of the country until 1935. The ancient Persians ruled an empire that stretched from the Indus River in India to the Nile River in Egypt. Over the centuries, this region became the prize of several conquerors—including the Greeks, the Parthians, the Sassanians, the Turks, and the Afghans. European powers, especially Great Britain and Russia, would play an important part in the country's development in the 1800s and early 1900s. The United States would also introduce Western ideas to Iran.

The twentieth century brought many important changes to Iran. In the late 1940s, after Iranian oil production became a successful industry, the government began a period of social and industrial change that brought its people needed reforms. By the 1970s, Iran had developed a strong capitalist market. But internal unrest made the government unstable. Clergy of the Islamic religion—the major faith in Iran—disagreed with the country's pro-Western direction.

A revolution in 1979 brought to power Ruhollah Khomeini, who held the titles ayatollah and wali faqih (chief religious and political leader). Khomeini turned the nation toward a conservative style of government based on Sharia (Islamic law).

Iran's sect of Islam—called Shiism—is central to the goals and decisions of the Iranian government. This religious emphasis is radically different from the beliefs of other Islamic countries, which are led by the Sunni sect of Islam. Most Arab states have rejected Iran's style of Islamic revolution, leading to Iran's isolation in the Middle East.

Religion has also brought Iran's regime into direct conflict with other Islamic nations, particularly its neighbor Iraq. The two countries also disagreed about oil rights and boundaries. Between 1980 and 1988, Iran and Iraq fought a bitter war. The war caused many deaths and weakened the oil economies of both countries. As a result of the hostilities, Iran lost oil markets and petroleum facilities.

In June 1989, Khomeini died without naming a successor. Voters elected Ali Akbar Hashemi Rafsanjani—speaker of the Iranian legislature—as the new president. With the support of the Iranian people and of the Islamic clergy, Rafsanjani established an ambitious five-year economic reform program.

Rafsanjani's reforms lost popular support during the early 1990s, however, and in 1997 Sayed Mohammad Khatami was elected president. Khatami promised to boost economic growth and to make social reforms. Despite these promises, few changes have actually been made. In addition, Khatami has drawn criticism from conservative Iranian leaders for his reforms.

SHIITES AND SUNNIS

Islam split into two sects soon after the death of its founder, the prophet Muhammad. Shiites believed that Muhammad's successor, or caliph, should be his closest male relative. This would have been his cousin and son-in-law Ali ibn Abi Talib. But Sunnis believed that the successor should be chosen from Muhammad's companions on the basis of his wisdom and faith.

Though Ali was not immediately chosen as caliph, he did become the fourth caliph in 656. But even then, Sunnis did not accept him. In 661 Ali was assassinated. His successor, Muawiyah, became the fifth caliph and the leader of the Sunnis. But the Shiites insisted that only Ali's descendants could be caliph.

In 2001, after terrorists attacked Washington, D.C., and New York City, U.S. president George W. Bush declared Iran a member of the "Axis of Evil," along with Iraq and North Korea. Bush claimed that these three countries are led by dangerous governments and that they probably possess weapons of mass destruction. (Weapons of mass destruction include chemical, biological, and nuclear arms that are capable of destroying large numbers of people at once.)

Outraged by this accusation, Iran's government in 2002 adamantly denied any link to the terrorist organization responsible for the attacks. Nevertheless, this label, as well as its economic woes, leaves Iran's future in an unstable position.

THE LAND

The Islamic Republic of Iran, situated in southwestern Asia, has an area of 636,296 square miles (1,648,007 square kilometers), making it more than twice the size of the state of Texas. Iran shares boundaries with seven nations and several bodies of water. The Caspian Sea lies to the north, as do the countries of Azerbaijan, Armenia, and Turkmenistan. Iraq and Turkey flank Iran to the west, and Pakistan and Afghanistan form the country's eastern border.

The nation's southern boundary lies along the Persian Gulf and the Gulf of Oman, which leads to the Arabian Sea. Among several islands that Iran has claimed is Qeshm, which is located in the Strait of Hormuz. The strait is a narrow channel that connects the Persian Gulf to the Gulf of Oman.

Topography

Iran is a land of many contrasts. Snowcapped mountains, ranging in height from 6,000 to 12,000 feet (1,829 to 3,658 meters), enclose a

rocky central plateau and arid salt deserts that support almost no life. A northern coastal strip along the Caspian Sea—the world's largest landlocked body of water—is the most fertile and most heavily populated region of the country. The Khuzestan Plain lies along a section of the Persian Gulf and contains Iran's rich bed of petroleum deposits.

Iran occupies the western and larger half of the great Plateau of Iran, a level region that links the steppes (semiarid grasslands) of Central Asia to the plateau of Asia Minor (mainland Turkey). The plateau is part of a larger topographical feature that extends eastward into Afghanistan and Pakistan. Underground plates of land have folded and pressed the edges of the landscape, forming several mountain ranges. As a result, Iran's topography has frequent fault lines, or seams, that move as pressure builds up beneath the earth. These movements often create devastating earthquakes.

Iran's section of the Plateau of Iran is triangular, and it is bounded by mountain chains. The Zagros Mountains lie in the west of the country.

The Dasht-e-Lut is a sand desert stretching 300 miles (480 km) long and 200 miles (320 km) wide. Iran's deserts, the Dasht-e-Lut and the Dasht-e-Kavir, together occupy most of the central portion of the Plateau of Iran.

Streams cut deep, narrow gorges through this range, carrying water to fertile valleys in the region. Much of the area is very rugged and is populated mostly by nomadic (seasonally wandering) peoples.

The Elburz range is located in the north and contains Mount Damavand (18,934 feet; 5,771 m), the highest peak in the nation. These mountains are made of volcanic rock and rise above the Caspian coastal strip. The mountains drop sharply from 10,000 feet (3,048 m) to the marshy water's edge. This lowland region once contained several shipping ports for traders crossing the Caspian Sea.

In the center of the Plateau of Iran is a great desert region that once formed the bed of a lake. Two deserts exist on the plateau, the Dasht-e-Kavir and the Dasht-e-Lut. The Dasht-e-Kavir in the north is unique because it is comprised of a crust of salt crystals instead of sand. Some forms of life grow in the Dasht-e-Kavir in areas where the soil is less salty and where oases (fertile areas) exist. To the south, the Dasht-e-Lut is a sand desert with sparse vegetation. Sandstorms frequently ravage the desert's landscape. Few explorers have ever dared to venture into the hostile wasteland of the Dasht-e-Lut.

At the northern end of the Persian Gulf, within Khuzestan Province, lies the plain that contains most of Iran's oil deposits. Tapped since 1908, the petroleum fields are clustered near Iran's eastern border with Iraq.

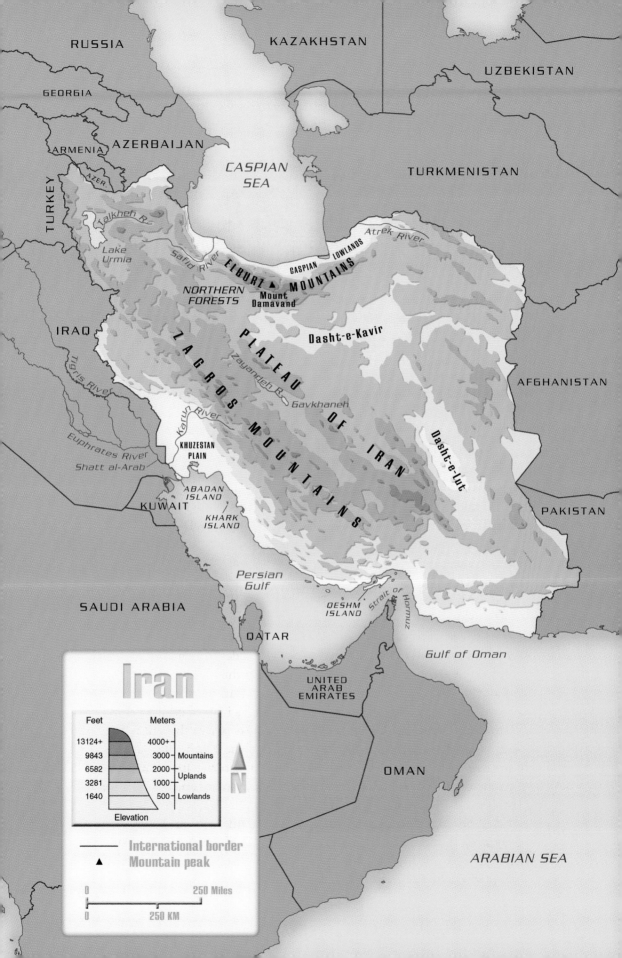

⊙ Bodies of Water

Water has always been a vital need on the Plateau of Iran. Three large rivers flow down from the mountains. The Safid River courses through the Elburz Mountains and into the Caspian Sea in northern Iran. Farther south, the Zayandeh River flows southeastward from the Zagros Mountains and drains into a swamp called Gavkhaneh in the Yazd region. The third major river—the Karun—is the only river in Iran that is navigable. It travels from the Zagros Mountains to the Shatt al-Arab—a narrow channel along the border with Iraq that marks the joining of the Tigris and Euphrates Rivers—and then flows into the Persian Gulf.

The great variation of water volume in Iran's rivers poses a major problem for the country's inhabitants. Streams fill with raging waters from rains and melted snow in the spring, only to become totally dry by late summer. Water remains underground, however, and Iranians have tapped groundwater supplies for irrigation since ancient times. During the mid-twentieth century, several large dams were built to reduce flooding, to conserve water, and to generate electricity.

The Caspian Sea, which is surrounded by Azerbaijan, Russia, Kazakhstan, Turkmenistan, and Iran, is entirely landlocked. The Caspian is the largest inland body of water on earth.

Qanats (a system of canals and wells) dot the Iranian landscape.

Other than the Caspian Sea, Iran has few inland bodies of water. Most result from seasonal rains and, consequently, dry up in the summertime. The Caspian Sea actually loses more water from evaporation than it receives from streams feeding into it. The country's largest permanent body of water lying completely within Iran is Lake Urmia in the northwest, near the city of Tabriz.

Climate

Like its topography, Iran's climate also has some extreme contrasts. In general, however, the climate of the northern and eastern parts is more moderate than the southern and western regions. Nevertheless, the capital city of Tehran, in northern Iran, has summer temperatures as high as 120°F (49°C) during the day.

Winter, especially from mid-December to mid-February, is severely cold, with snow, ice, and below-zero temperatures. Iran's spring is short and often rainy. Autumn is long, with sunny days and cool nights.

The area around Tehran sees some of the country's most extreme weather. Summers are hot and dry, and winter temperatures often drop below freezing (Fahrenheit)—especially at night. The central plateau receives about 15 inches (38 centimeters) of precipitation annually and is considered semiarid. The Zagros range averages about 25 inches (64 cm), some of it in the form of snow.

The region with the most temperate year-round climate is the narrow, lush strip of land between the Elburz Mountains and the Caspian Sea. The region near the Caspian Sea receives between 40 and 60 inches (102 and 152 cm) of rain throughout the year.

The area around the Persian Gulf is the hottest in Iran, and temperatures can rise to more than 120°F (49°C) in summer. This factor, plus high humidity, makes summers hard for people living in the gulf area. Despite high humidity, rain is rare, and annual precipitation is between 3 to 5 inches (7.6 cm to 13 cm).

The west, especially in the area that is close to Turkey, receives more rain and snow at the higher elevations. Lower elevations—close to the Iraqi border—are known for their hot climate.

Flora and Fauna

The northern part of Iran, where some of the world's finest walnut trees grow, contains the last remaining thickly forested area of the Middle East. At the foot of the Elburz Mountains lies a region dotted with oak, willow, fig, and pomegranate trees. Orange, lemon, and date trees also grow in this area, as well as in other parts of the country.

One of Iran's most important trees is the pistachio—prized for its nuts and also for its wood—which is widespread in the northern part of the country. In the south, date trees surround streams and oases. These trees are frequently seen along the border with Iraq and on the Shatt al-Arab. Scrub vegetation and cacti dominate the landscape of the arid central plateau. Southern and eastern Iran have sparse vegetation, with the exception of some scattered juniper trees. Palm trees grow on the country's southern coastal lowland and around the lush desert oases.

The pistachio tree is well suited to Iran's climate, because it can withstand hot and cold temperatures. Pistachio trees produce nuts for several hundred years.

The **frog-eyed sand gecko** makes its home in Iran's deserts. The country's lake and sea coastlines offer habitats for **pelicans.**

Iran has several varieties of natural flora, including grasses, fruit tree blossoms, and wildflowers. The most common wildflowers include wild irises and poppies, several varieties of crocus, and the Shiraz grape.

The northern forests provide habitats for tigers, panthers, wolves, foxes, and bears. Rabbits, jackals, deer, and badgers are also fairly common. Inland and in the south live some of Iran's abundant birdlife, including pheasants, pelicans, partridges, and flamingos. Wild goats and sheep inhabit the southern mountains. The Caspian Sea and its inlets host many varieties of fish, such as sturgeon, whitefish, and herring. Reptiles are commonly found in the deserts, especially snakes and lizards.

Environmental Issues

Despite unforgiving deserts and sparsely populated mountains, Iran is home to more than ten thousand species of plants, many of which exist only in Iran. Only about one hundred species of mammals live in Iran, with about 20 percent of these native to the country. And nearly five hundred species of birds have been recorded in the country. Unfortunately, many of these unique creatures face the possibility of extinction.

POLLUTING THE PERSIAN GULF

Since the discovery of oil in Iran in the early twentieth century, the Persian Gulf has played an important role in the country's oil industry. Not surprisingly, the gulf suffers from massive, unchecked pollution. Oil spills and unregulated industrial development on the gulf islands have damaged the gulf's unique ecosystem. The Iran-Iraq War (1980–1988) was particularly devastating to the area as more than 200,000 tons (181,436 metric tons) of oil spilled from oil rigs. In addition, sewage, garbage, and toxic chemicals have all been dumped into the gulf, further polluting its waters.

Oil slicks in the Persian Gulf *(below)* hurt marine life and coastal wildlife.

Industrial and urban development are big challenges to Iran's environment. The coastline along the Caspian Sea has been especially ravaged by unplanned urban sprawl. Air and water pollution in the area have actually increased since the 1990s, threatening wetlands and their wildlife.

In the north, smog from factories and exhaust from vehicles has created an air pollution problem for Tehran. And oil leaks from rigs and tankers, as well as untreated sewage, have contaminated the once unsoiled Persian Gulf. Years of conflict with Iraq also resulted in heavy damage to the environment.

Another important environmental problem for Iran is massive deforestation. Since the 1960s and 1970s, about 321,236 acres (130,000 hectares) of northern forest have been cleared by the timber industry and for urban and agricultural development.

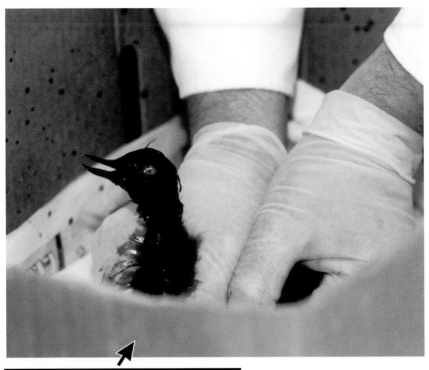

A conservation worker cleans off a bird rescued from an oil spill in the Persian Gulf. Oil slicks devastate the gulf long after cleanup.

Iran's environmental problems are worsened by natural disasters such as earthquakes. The country's volcanic mountains make Iran an active earthquake zone. Northwestern Iran, which contain some of the Elburz and Zagros Mountains, is particularly prone to devastating earthquakes. In 1990 the worst earthquake to hit Iran claimed the lives of 45,000 people. In addition to loss of life, the quakes may cause oil spills and fires, which in turn damage the country's environment.

This loss of habitat threatens the country's flora and fauna. In addition, the loss of trees and the overgrazing of livestock have left the land open to erosion, which hurts the country's farmers.

The Iranian government has started several conservation programs to help protect the country's resources. A reforestation program is working to replant nearly 10 million acres (4 million hectares) of forest. And the government established the Environmental Protection Organization to create and enforce conservation laws. In addition, the creation of national parks and wildlife preserves helps to preserve the native flora and fauna.

By 2000, for example, Iran had established eighty-six protected wildlife reserves.

Despite these efforts, however, Iran's environment still faces many challenges. Limited resources make it difficult to enforce conservation laws. Many conservationists believe that environmental protection remains low on the country's priority list.

Cities

About 66 percent of Iran's 65.6 million people live in urban areas. Many Iranians moved to the cities beginning in the mid-twentieth century, when large-scale urban modernization offered the promise of better jobs.

TEHRAN (population 6.8 million) lies in northern Iran. The city is the nation's most important industrial and cultural hub, as well as the largest urban area in the country. The capital of Iran since 1789, the city underwent extensive modernization during the twentieth century. Skyscrapers and modern boulevards have been built near ancient mosques (Islamic houses of prayer), and narrow, winding streets are common.

Tehran, Iran's capital city, features a mixture of ancient and modern architecture.

Visit vgsbooks.com, where you'll find links to photographs and information on current weather conditions, the most up-to-date population figures and other statistics, ancient sites to explore in Tehran and other places, and items of interest.

MASHHAD (population 1.9 million) became of strategic importance in the nineteenth and twentieth centuries because of it lay between Russia and Afghanistan. But the city—which lies in the rich agricultural region of Khorasan Province—had been a major trade center between India and Persia for centuries. In addition, Mashhad has become a religious site for Shiite Muslims.

ESFAHAN (population 1.3 million) is Iran's third largest city and served as Persia's capital in the sixteenth century. Shah (king) Abbas I built several noteworthy mosques throughout his long reign, and Esfahan still shows the beauty of traditional Islamic architecture. Industrial products made in Esfahan include textiles and steel.

TABRIZ (population 1.2 million) was the capital of Persia in the fifteenth century. Modern Tabriz is the main urban center of northwestern Iran. Tabriz became a junction for roads and railways during the Russian occupation of the early and mid-twentieth century. Carpets, leather goods, soap, and dried fruits are among Tabriz's important products. The city has suffered frequently from earthquake damage and foreign occupation.

SHIRAZ (population 1 million), in central Iran, was an important commercial center until the early 1930s. The modern city is an administrative center for Fars Province. Many people consider Shiraz to be the heartland of Persian culture, and the city's most famous buildings have been restored to celebrate its past glory. The city also lies near the ruins of Persepolis, which served as the capital of the ancient Persian Empire from 559 to 330 B.C.

HISTORY AND GOVERNMENT

The earliest archaeological evidence of human beings in Iran dates from 100,000 years ago. These early nomads—people who moved seasonally to follow herds of animals that they hunted—left no written records.

The first recorded culture in Iran was organized by the Elamites, who were living in the southwest by about 3000 B.C. By about 1000 B.C., two Aryan peoples—the Medes and the Persians—had wandered down through Central Asia and had formed two different nations in the territory of present-day Iran. (The word Aryan would later give Iran its name.)

The Medes lived in the northwest and called their realm Media. The Persians settled in southern Iran. The Greek name for the region was Persis, from which Persia is derived. Starting as a small kingdom in the foothills of southwestern Iran, the Persian Empire became a world power. In the span of two generations, Persia's leaders pushed the boundaries of the empire far beyond Iran.

○ The Persians

In 553 B.C., the Persians led by Cyrus the Great subdued the Medes and annexed Media to Persia. Cyrus was a member of the Achaemenid dynasty (family of rulers), named after an earlier Persian leader. Cyrus conquered lands that stretched from modern Greece to modern Pakistan and built his capital at Pasargadae.

At its peak, the empire eventually stretched as far eastward as modern-day Pakistan and as far westward as Libya. Persia extended from the Aral Sea in the north to the Gulf of Oman in the south. Later Achaemenids developed vast systems of overland travel, expanded opportunities for trade, and established their capital city at Persepolis, near present-day Shiraz. By the end of the sixth century, however, it became evident that the fast-growing empire did not have a stable foundation. This was, in part, because Cyrus's successors could not decide on how to choose a new leader. In addition, a series of rebellions, called the Persian Wars, broke out.

By 522 B.C., Darius sat on the Persian throne. He stopped one of the worst revolts—a Greek revolt in Asia Minor (modern Turkey) in 494 B.C.—but the Greeks defeated other Persian expeditions at Marathon and Salamis. Darius died in 486 B.C. without renewing the battle against Greece.

Darius's successors were unable to hold Persia together, and the empire broke apart into several kingdoms. At the same time, the Greek city-state of Macedonia, led by Philip of Macedon, grew more powerful and set its sights on Persia. Philip's son Alexander the Great led an army against Persia starting in 334 B.C. He defeated Persia's troops at Issus in 333 B.C., and two years later, the Persians lost a final battle to Alexander's forces at Gaugamela.

For Persia the arrival of Alexander signaled the beginning of foreign rule. Alexander's goal was to unite the Greek and Persian civilizations into a single unit. But Alexander's untimely death in 323 B.C. left his empire in disarray since he had no heirs. Alexander's empire became divided into small, local kingdoms, as his generals competed for ultimate control.

DARIUS THE GREAT

Legend surrounds the ascension of Darius I, also known as Darius the Great, to the Persian throne. After the mysterious death of the previous ruler in 522, a small group of nobles decided that the new ruler should be chosen by the gods. They agreed that the owner of the first horse to whinny at dawn would be their new leader. Darius's horse was the first to utter a sound—with a little help from his groom. As king, Darius reestablished the fractured empire and managed to expand its borders to India in the east and to the Danube River in the north.

Persian ruler Darius III (right, top center) at the Battle of Issus (333 B.C.). Darius lost the battle with the Greeks, and Persian control of the Mediterranean region declined.

Seleucus, one of Alexander's generals, took control of the territory of present-day Iran and founded the Seleucid dynasty. The Seleucids governed the area until about 250 B.C., when troops from Parthia, a kingdom south of the Caspian Sea, conquered the Selecuid lands.

The Parthians ruled Persia for almost five hundred years. They adopted much of Greek culture but also encouraged a return to Persian traditions and customs. The Parthians also expanded Persia's boundaries into India and to the frontiers of Egypt. But in A.D. 224, the Sassanians, a local dynasty centered in Fars Province, overthrew the Parthians. Sassanian kings ruled Persian lands from the third to the seventh centuries A.D. The Sassanians made Zoroastrianism, a Persian faith whose followers believed in one god, the empire's official religion.

Foreign Rulers

Ineffective rulers and constant border wars contributed to the downfall of the Sassanian Empire. Persia became an easy target for an Arab army that came from present-day Saudi Arabia. Motivating these fighters was a new faith—Islam—that called for the expansion of territory and for the conversion of non-Islamic peoples. Under their Islamic leader, called a caliph, Arab forces defeated the Sassanians in the mid-seventh century. Muslims (followers of Islam) carried their Islamic ideas with them and installed Islam as the national religion. Persia quickly converted to Islam.

In the seventh century, soon after the death of Muhammad, the founder and leader of the Islamic religion, a controversy emerged over how to choose his successors. As a result, two Islamic sects—the Sunnis and the Shiites—developed. Sunnis supported an elected Islamic leadership, while Shiites believed the only true successors to Muhammad were his descendants.

Most Persian groups belonged to the Shiite sect, although their Arab rulers followed the Sunni sect. In 750 Shiites rebelled against the Sunni rulers and established the Abbasid dynasty.

Abbasid rulers established their capital at Baghdad, in modern Iraq, and ruled Persia for more than a century. During this time, a number of small kingdoms also emerged under different rulers.

Another group—the nomadic Seljuk Turks from Central Asia—began moving into Persia. They united various local kingdoms and established their capital just south of modern Tehran. At its height, the Seljuk Empire stretched from the Mediterranean Sea to the Gobi Desert in Central Asia.

During more than a century of Seljuk rule, the arts and sciences thrived. After the death of the Seljuk leader Malik-Shah, however, rivalries divided the Seljuk Empire. The weakened realm attracted a new invading force—the Mongols from China.

Sweeping through China in the thirteenth century, the Mongols and their leader Genghis Khan (meaning "world conqueror") made their way to the territory of present-day Iran. With a strong and well-trained army, the Mongols conquered the remainder of the Seljuk Empire. Mongol soldiers destroyed cities and towns, killing thousands of people.

Although they were harsh military conquerors, the Mongols opened trade between Persia and Asia. They also introduced Chinese artisanship to Persian art.

One of the last Mongol khans, Timur the Lame, arrived in Persia from the north in 1380. Timur established a strong empire, but his death in 1405 resulted in internal rivalry over the throne. This infighting weakened the dynasty and eventually brought an end to Mongol rule in Persia in the mid-fifteenth century.

◑ The Safavid Shahs

During the fifteenth and sixteenth centuries, several local dynasties began to take control of parts of Iran. One of these was the Safavids, who lived in eastern Azerbaijan. By 1500 the Safavid leader Esmail had taken Tabriz and had proclaimed the Shiite sect of Islam to be the state religion.

A powerful neighbor, the Ottoman Empire, advanced eastward from Asia Minor into Persia. Tabriz fell, and Esmail's successor moved the Safavid capital to the shelter of Qazvin near the Elburz Mountains. From this location, the kingdom began to prosper.

The Safavid shah Abbas I ruled Persia from 1587 to 1629. After moving the capital from Qazvin to Esfahan in 1598, Abbas transformed the site from an underdeveloped city into one of the most beautiful capitals of its day.

Abbas's reign saw a renewal of the arts. Persian textiles—including carpets, silks, and brocades—calligraphy (ornate handwriting), and bookbinding flourished. Mosques of unique beauty and artistry were built and adorned with fine ceramics and mosaic tiles.

The Royal Mosque in Esfahan. This mosque was one of many architectural creations built from 1587 to 1629, during the rule of **Shah Abbas I** *(inset).*

The Safavid dynasty fell in 1722, when Afghan forces looking to expand their territory surrounded the Safavid capital of Esfahan. Afghan rule ended in 1727, after they were defeated in several battles by a Persian force led by Nader Qoli. Soon after his victories, Nader proclaimed himself shah of Persia. Organizing an expedition, he conquered Afghanistan and then marched eastward to Delhi, India.

Nader became a cruel tyrant, however, and his rule included huge tax demands and misuse of the land. In 1747 a captain of his own guard assassinated him. A successor to Nader, Karim Khan Zand Mohammad, ruled peacefully for twenty-five years, healing the wounds of constant conflict. But the death of Karim Khan in 1779 left the empire in turmoil as internal rivalries fought for the throne.

◉ Outside Influence

In 1794 the Qajars, a Turkish group that had settled in the north around the Caspian Sea, took control of the Persian Empire. But at the start of the nineteenth century, Qajar rulers were forced to deal with new threats—Russia and Britain.

Both world powers had strong interests in the area. The British wanted to protect their trade routes to India, while the Russians wanted to push into Persian territory. Russian rulers were expanding into the Caucasus Mountains, an area historically linked to Persia.

This decorative tile shows **Nasir al-Din Shah** *(right)* fighting a duel in the mid-1800s. A skilled warrior and politician, the leader still could not stop Britain and Russia from taking control of Persia.

The Russians and Qajars waged war from 1797 to 1834, which proved disastrous for Persia. The Qajar rulers ceded all their claims in Central Asia to the Russians. By 1857 British forces had taken over all of Persia's claims to territories in present-day Afghanistan.

Nasir al-Din Shah, who ruled the Qajar dynasty from 1848 to 1896, embraced European science and technology. European educational ideas and industry were introduced to Persia, and the shah worked to modernize the empire. But soon Britain began to play a role in Persia's trade and political system. The Qajar dynasty gave the British the right to form the Imperial Bank of Persia and to explore for oil. The British struck oil in 1908. The Anglo-Persian Oil Company was founded in 1909, and Britain began expanding its control over the area.

This rise of foreign influence caused groups of Persians to seek changes. In the early twentieth century, merchants, members of the Islamic clergy, and political reformists joined forces to demand that the shah agree to a constitution and a national assembly, called the Majlis.

The Qajars took a neutral stance in World War I (1914–1918), but this did not prevent Persia from being occupied by Russian and British troops. In postwar peace conferences, it appeared that Britain would dominate Persia's future. In 1919 the Qajar shah signed the Anglo-Persian Treaty, making the country a British protectorate.

A coup d'état (a sudden change of government) in 1921 prevented the treaty from being put into practice. Reza Khan, a general in the Persian cavalry who strongly objected to Persia becoming a foreign country's protectorate, led the coup. By 1923 he had become prime minister, and the last Qajar shah had left the country. In 1926 a special assembly chose Reza Khan—renamed Reza Shah Pahlavi—as the head of a new Persian dynasty.

Reza Shah and World War II

Appalled by Persia's underdevelopment, Reza Shah set out to bring European ways and technology to the nation. Through modernization, Reza Shah hoped to put Persia back on the road to greatness. He ordered Persian men to replace their traditional clothes with European suits and Persian women to take off their veils. These changes caused the clergy to resist the shah's modernization plans. New laws also permitted women to go to the movies and to visit cafés for the first time.

In 1935 the shah changed the official name of the country to Iran (from the word Aryan, the name of Iran's early settlers), and he cut Arabic and Turkish words from Farsi, the Persian language.

Reza Shah Pahlavi

World War II broke out in 1939, and Iran again became a battleground for foreign troops. Frustrated by British interference in Iran, Reza Shah allied himself with the Axis powers of Germany, Italy, and later Japan. These countries fought against the Allied powers of Britain, the United States, and the Soviet Union (which included Russia). In 1941 British and Soviet troops occupied Iran and forced the shah to give up the throne to his son, Mohammed. Reza Shah was deported to South Africa.

During the war, Iran served as a vital link in the Allied supply line to the Soviet Union. In 1943 Franklin Roosevelt from the United States, Winston Churchill from Great Britain, and Joseph Stalin from the Soviet Union met in Tehran to discuss military action against Germany. The talks also included ideas about postwar politics. The document they created at the meeting, the Tehran Declaration, set forth many future plans, including Iran's independence.

Under the terms of the declaration, foreign troops were to be withdrawn by 1946. Soviet forces in northern Iran, however, refused to leave.

The Soviets also supported pro-Soviet rebels. The Iranian government, backed by the United Nations (UN) and strongly supported by the United States, expelled the Soviet army. The young shah, Mohammed Reza Pahlavi, took up the reins of power and appointed Mohammad Mosaddeq prime minister and leader of the Majlis. Iran and its young ruler were finally free from foreign rule.

Mohammed Reza Pahlavi

In the postwar era, the oil rights that Iran had sold to foreign companies grew in importance and value. U.S. and British oil companies were asking for further oil drilling rights in southeastern Iran, and the Soviet Union was requesting rights in the north. The Majlis rejected both of these requests in order to limit the amount of foreign influence on Iran's affairs. Supported by the Majlis, Mosaddeq nationalized (changed to government ownership) the British-run oil industry in Iran. The prime minister also sponsored a law that removed the oil industry from British control. Most British citizens left Iran, and the huge British-built refinery in the city of Abadan, located on Abadan Island in the Shatt al-Arab, was closed. As a result, production of oil fell drastically, and widespread unemployment and unrest occurred.

Because of the internal unrest, Mosaddeq asked the shah for unlimited control of the government. The shah refused and named a new prime minister. Faced with public rioting at the removal of Mosaddeq, however, the shah reappointed him, giving Mosaddeq the requested powers. In 1952 the prime minister authorized laws to strictly censor news, to prohibit labor strikes, and to suspend elections to the Majlis. Economic difficulties increased, partly because U.S. and European oil companies refused to buy Iranian oil.

Mohammed Reza Pahlavi

Support for Mosaddeq waned in the Majlis, which he tried to abolish, and in 1953 the shah dismissed him. Mosaddeq refused to relinquish his office and announced that he had overthrown the shah. The shah left Iran, and riots and unrest spread throughout Tehran for four days.

The army supported the return of the shah and arrested Mosaddeq and his followers. British and U.S. agencies both secretly and openly assisted the army, ensuring the success of the shah's forces against Mosaddeq. The shah returned to Tehran, and Fazlollah Zahedi became prime minister. No longer having to compete with Mosaddeq for power, Mohammad Reza Pahlavi began to centralize his authority and to diminish the power of the Majlis.

In the late 1950s, the shah instituted the first of several methods to maintain his authority. He created a national security and intelligence organization called SAVAK (Sazamane Atelaat Va Amniate Kechvar), which monitored political activity and the press. Arrests and torture of prisoners by SAVAK agents were frequent and caused a high degree of antigovernment feeling among various elements of Iranian society. An elite group of military and civilian employees remained faithful to the shah, who rewarded their loyalty with large salaries.

In 1962 the shah declared a land reform and redistribution plan, called the White Revolution. Land was taken out of the hands of large landowners, who then could no longer fine their tenants by collecting most of the harvests as rents. In addition, electoral reform was enacted, and Iranian women voted for the first time in 1963. Later, the government made efforts to increase the literacy rate and to improve health standards.

But sudden attempts to modernize and Westernize Iran drew criticism from traditional landowners and from Shiite leaders, including the Ayatollah Ruhollah Khomeini, who was an outspoken opponent of the shah's reforms. In 1963 the shah's forces attacked the headquarters of the Islamic clergy near the city of Qom and arrested Khomeini. The next day, demonstrations against Khomeini's imprisonment erupted in Tehran and other cities. A year later, Khomeini was freed, and he left the country, moving first to Iraq and then to France.

The 1960s and 1970s were decades of economic growth and wider international involvement for Iran. Iran sought to establish alliances with many other countries, developing close links with the Soviet Union. Iran also joined many Arab nations to help establish the Organization of Petroleum Exporting Countries (OPEC). Member-countries of OPEC work together on issues that mutually benefit them, including setting the price of oil exports.

◉ Becoming an Islamic Republic

To centralize his authority further, the shah banned oppositional political parties in 1975. The shah's response to the resulting internal dissatisfaction became increasingly repressive, and human rights organizations reported numerous violations, carried out mostly by members of SAVAK.

Meanwhile, the vast oil profits coming to Iran paid for internal development projects and strengthened Iran's position abroad. The population continued to increase, and thousands moved from rural to urban areas, especially to the capital. Among traditional Shiite Islamic groups, a feeling prevailed that plans for development and modernization were growing too rapidly. Demonstrations erupted against the government in 1978, and Iran was on the verge of civil war by late autumn.

In late 1978, the shah declared martial law, or military rule, and his forces attacked protesters in downtown Tehran. This proved ineffective, however. Unable to rule, the shah departed for Egypt, leaving the government in the hands of his prime minister. On February 1, 1979, Ruhollah Khomeini returned to Iran from exile and appointed Mehdi Bazargan, a moderate civilian, as the prime minister of an Islamic revolutionary government.

A national public vote held in April 1979 enabled Khomeini to establish a Shiite Islamic republic and eventually to enact a new constitution. Khomeini became Iran's first wali faqih, the country's chief Islamic religious scholar and leader. The regime executed many members of SAVAK and other supporters of the shah. Organized according to Islamic ideals, the government repealed the modern divorce laws and again required women to wear the chador, or veil, in accordance with Islamic law. The new leaders suppressed Western influences, and many Western-educated Iranians fled the country.

Islamic fundamentalists loyal to the **Ayatollah Ruhollah Khomeini** *(top left)* welcome the religious leader back to Iran after his return from exile in 1979.

Iranian terrorists, angry with U.S. support of the exiled shah, seize the U.S. embassy in Tehran in 1979. The terrorists took sixty-six Americans hostage.

The establishment of the Islamic Republic strained Iranian and U.S. relations. The situation came to a head in September 1979, when the exiled shah was admitted to the United States for medical treatment. In response, on November 4, 1979, Iranian terrorists took over the U.S. embassy in Tehran and took sixty-six Americans hostage. The act was said to be a response to continued U.S. support for the shah, who died in Egypt in 1980. Fifty-two of the hostages were held for 444 days and were eventually released on January 20, 1981.

Conflict with Iraq

Iran also experienced conflicts with its neighbors. Iran and Iraq had long disagreed about access to the Shatt al-Arab and about the ownership of several islands in the gulf. In 1980 the Iraqi government demanded independence for a Sunni Muslim minority in Khuzestan in southwestern Iran. The Iranian government rejected these demands, and in September 1980, Iraqi forces invaded the province. By the end of the year, Iranian troop advances had produced a stalemate with the Iraqi forces. The conflict continued, causing regional and international concern over the threat to oil resources and to governments in the Persian Gulf area.

In the mid-1980s, the war still received public support in Iran, in part because Iranians regarded the conflict as one between the Shiite and Sunni branches of Islam. In addition, Iranian troops had successfully captured Iraqi territory near the Shatt al-Arab, hampering Iraq's ability to export oil, and, therefore, to finance its military activities.

Arab states in the region watched the war from the sidelines and feared that Iran would export its radical-style Shiite Islamic government to their own countries.

Beginning in 1987, Iran experienced some setbacks. Frequent bombings of Iranian oil tankers and other ships occurred in the gulf. Armed forces from other nations—notably those of the United States—cooperated with neutral Arab states to protect vessels trying to pass through the gulf. On several occasions, U.S. and Iranian forces clashed in the region, resulting in property damage and loss of life for both sides.

The Arab League (an organization of Arab nations dedicated to strengthening Arab unity) called for Iran and Iraq to accept a UN-sponsored cease-fire. Iraq, which was militarily weak at that point, consented to the resolution, but Iran did not. As a result, support for Iran within the Arab world weakened.

Iran launched a new offensive in 1988, but by the middle of the year, it lacked sufficient weaponry and troop enlistments to continue the war. Khomeini took the advice of his top officials, including legislative spokesperson Ali Akbar Hashemi Rafsanjani, and accepted the UN resolution for a cease-fire. The measure included arrangements both for troop withdrawals and for the exchange of prisoners of war.

◉ Problems and Reforms

Throughout the 1980s, Iran's economy suffered due to war and internal problems. Iran was forced to import food and weapons, and these import costs further drained the nation's financial reserves.

A **mural** in Tehran honors Iranian heroes. Along with soldiers of the Iran-Iraq War, religious leaders Ali Khamenei *(top left)* and Ayatollah Ruhollah Khomeini *(top right)* and political leader Ali Akbar Hashemi Rafsanjani *(bottom right)* are featured prominently.

Iran suffered on the international scene as well, as Iranian militant groups supported terrorist actions around the world, including the capture in Lebanon of hostages from the United States and Europe. These actions by some Iranians damaged Iran's global reputation.

Rivalry among political groups continued to weaken the unity of the government in the late 1980s. When the ayatollah died in June 1989, he left a huge gap in the religious and political leadership. Within hours of his death, an Islamic council named Ali Khamenei as the new supreme spiritual authority. In national elections held in July, voters chose Rafsanjani to replace Khamenei as the next president of Iran.

With the backing both of the Iranian people and of the Islamic clergy, Khamenei and Rafsanjani began working to improve the economy and foreign relations. In 1989 President Rafsanjani established a five-year economic reform program, which included foreign borrowing and foreign investment. As a result, throughout the early 1990s, the government worked to improve its international reputation and to restore relations with many nations.

But conflicts in the area still affected Iran. In August 1990, Iraq invaded Kuwait. This action caused the United Nations to impose economic sanctions on Iraq. The United States, as well as countries in Europe and the Middle East, sent troops to the region to protect the nations that border Iraq. In January 1991, the United States and its allies declared war on Iraq. Although Iran did not send troops to fight in the war, the Iranian government publicly denounced Iraq's actions and supported the economic sanctions throughout the war. In late 1991, the Iranian government also assisted in the release of the hostages in Lebanon. These actions helped improve Iran's foreign relations and to repair the country's global reputation.

Rafsanjani and his moderate policies took control of the parliament through elections in 1992. But Rafsanjani's attempts at liberal reforms were effectively blocked by the conservative religious minority that remained in the government. To complicate matters, in 1996 the United States banned all trade with Iran, alleging that the country supported international terrorism. This further hurt an already ailing economy.

In 1997 Sayed Mohammad Khatami, a moderate reformist, was elected president of the republic. Despite conservative cleric opposition, Khatami emphasized a goal of balancing growth in the political, economic, and social arenas. He also pledged to promote individual rights. Following his election, a border crossing opened between Iraq and Iran, the first since the Iran-Iraq War. Khatami made strides in the political arena, replacing many local governors with his reformers.

Despite reforms, however, conservatives in the legislature voted in 1999 to limit the press, forcing several liberal newspapers to close. University students promoting democratic reforms demonstrated in Tehran, and mass riots later started after police raided dormitories and killed as many as eight students. Order was restored after five days of rioting and about 1,400 arrests.

The start of the new millennium was not without problems. In 2000 Iran's southern region suffered its worst drought in thirty years, forcing the government to ration water. People in several cities protested against water and electricity shortages that same month.

While Khatami has received criticism from both liberals and conservatives, a majority reelected him in June 2001. Relations between Iran and the United States, which have been strained since the 1950s, seemed to improve slightly in 2001. When President Bush included Iran in his Axis of Evil, however, tension between the two nations rose again.

Internal problems continued to plague Iran's political system in 2002 and 2003. President Khatami, determined to balance Islamic ideals within a democratic system, worked to prevent the government's constitutional violations, such as trying and executing political prisoners without a jury. Khatami drafted a bill intended to prevent or reverse these actions. He also began working on a second bill that seeks to limit the power of certain conservative councils, which have the right to disqualify reformist candidates from office.

Despite these efforts, however, the future of these reforms remains questionable. Reelections will take place in 2004, and politicians from

Iranian students demonstrate for democratic reforms and for an end to government censorship.

both conservative and reformist camps believe that the Ayatollah Ali Khamenei will disqualify most reformist candidates. This move will once again place the regime in the hands of the conservatives.

Government

Iran's constitution, which was adopted in 1979 and revised in 1989, establishes Iran as an Islamic republic. Islamic ideals serve as the basis for political, social, and economic order.

Iran is governed by both secular and religious leaders. The chief ruler is a religious leader who carries the title wali faqih. He is an expert scholar well versed in Islamic ideas and the law of the Quran. The Quran is the sacred book of Islamic writings that holds the teachings of the prophet Muhammad. The wali faqih holds powers and rights that outweigh those of any appointed or elected government official. Many religious leaders also hold positions in the various government branches.

The president acts as chief executive of the country. Although elected by direct vote to a four-year term, the president does not rule the country independently of the wali faqih and other Islamic leaders. The president appoints the Council of Ministers, makes government decisions, and selects which policies will go to the Majlis.

Legislative power rests with the Majlis, whose members are directly elected by the Iranian people. The 290 representatives serve four-year terms and may increase in number as the population grows. A Council of Guardians reviews all legislation from the Majlis to make certain that laws do not contradict the Quran. This twelve-member council consists of six clergy appointed by the wali faqih and six lawyers appointed by the legislature.

A supreme court and a judicial council carry out the laws of the land. These two separate groups share judicial responsibilities and a single leader. The judicial council strictly enforces Islamic laws, or Sharia.

For administrative purposes, the country is divided into twenty-eight provinces called *ostans*. District officials, appointed by the central government, share the day-to-day job of local administration. Provincial councils, called *anjumans*, also ensure that citizens and government officials are following Islamic laws.

CRIME AND PUNISHMENT

Iran's criminal justice system is often perceived by other nations as harsh. For example, adultery is punishable by death. In 2001 a woman who was convicted of murder and adultery was stoned to death in a Tehran prison. Another form of execution is public hanging. Crimes such as drinking alcohol and socializing with women who are not family may be punished by public floggings (whippings).

THE PEOPLE

Iranians represent many ancestries. Most Iranians are of Persian descent and speak Farsi, an Indo-European language. Iran includes sizable Turkish and Arab minorities, who speak Turkish and Arabic dialects, as well as ethnic groups such as the Kurds, the Lur, and the Baluchi, who also speak Indo-European languages.

With 65.6 million people, Iran has a population density of about 104 persons per square mile (40 per sq. km). About 35 percent of the people live in small villages scattered throughout the countryside, while more than 65 percent make their homes in Iran's cities.

Iranian cities typically have an older, established section and a modern section. The older sections are often characterized by mosques and open-air markets, where merchants sell food and hand-made goods. The modern parts of Iranian cities include hospitals and schools, as well as offices and restaurants. Most city dwellers live in apartment buildings or in small mud-brick buildings that stand around a central courtyard.

The villages of rural Iranians usually have a central village square. Typically, the square features a mosque and a public bath. Larger villages may have a clinic and a small school. Families living in the country usually make their homes in mud-brick houses with thatched roofs. Rural homes often have only one or two rooms and rarely have electricity or running water. Iranians who live in rural areas typically have little furniture. Traditionally, they use cushions to sit on and mattresses for sleeping.

Iranian nomads, people who travel from place to place to graze their livestock, live in round black tents. Nomads use donkeys and camels to carry all their possessions with them.

◉ Ethnic Groups

Although the term Persian has been widely used to refer to all of Iran's population, the name best describes a group of people who speak Indo-Aryan dialects and who are considered the direct descendants of the

Aryans who migrated to Iran from Central Asia. Persians make up about 60 percent of Iran's population. Most ethnic Persians live in Tehran, Esfahan, Shiraz, and other cities and villages in the northern and western plateau.

The Azeri form Iran's second largest ethnic group with about 24 percent of the population. The Azeri live mostly in the northwest, and they retain close cultural ties to ethnic Azeri in neighboring countries. They are descended from Turkish peoples who settled the area around Azerbaijan.

The Kurds form 7 percent of the total number of Iranians. The Kurds reside mainly in the Zagros Mountains of northwestern Iran. Language and ethnic customs relate the Kurds to the Persians, although scientists consider them to be descendants of the original Medes. The Kurds have resisted becoming part of modern nations, believing that they should be allowed to freely cross borders with their livestock herds. After the 1979 Shiite revolution, the Sunni Kurds demanded independence, and only recently have relations eased between the government and the Kurdish religious minority.

A small number of Arabs also live in Iran, making up 3 percent of the country's population. The Arabs are concentrated in Khuzestan

Persian boys wait in a schoolyard. Persians make up more than half of Iran's population.

(At right) a young **Turkoman woman** weaves a rug using a pattern exclusive to her people. This mother and child are **Iranian Kurds.**

Province, in southwestern Iran, and on the Persian Gulf islands. Many Iranian Arabs work in the oil industry and retain ties with relatives living in Iraq and Saudi Arabia.

The Lur, Baloch, and Turkoman groups each make up about 2 percent of Iran's population. The Lur live in the west near the Iraqi border. The closest of any present-day Iranians to the original Central Asian settlers, the Lur are divided between year-round residents of villages and migratory herders. Also nomadic and related to the Lur are the Bakhtiaris, who live in the area stretching from Lorestan to Khuzestan near the Iraqi border. Most Turkomans live in Mazandaran and Khorasan Provinces, close to Turkmenistan. They speak their own Turkic language. The Baloch are seminomadic and occupy the desert regions of southeastern Iran.

NOMADS

Several groups of nomadic people live in Iran, including the Kurds, the Baloch, and the Bakhtiari. While these groups have adapted to many of the country's customs, they proudly retain differences. The most important difference is the social role of women. Women in nomadic groups often have more freedom and higher status than Persian women. Nomadic women do not usually wear veils, and they are allowed to socialize freely with men. Some even lead their clans.

Iranian Muslims believe in twelve imams (religious leaders). According to Shiism, these twelve were the only men entrusted to interpret the Quran. Eleven of the imams died, and the twelfth imam simply disappeared in 878. Because of this, he is often called the Hidden Imam. The government makes decisions in his name.

Iran also supports a large number of refugees (people who are forced to flee their homeland due to war or persecution). In 1992 approximately 2 million Afghan refugees had trekked to Iran. While many had started returning to their homes by 1993, by 1999 Iran was still sheltering about 1.8 million refugees, more than any other country.

⊙ Religion

Ninety-eight percent of Iranians are Muslims. After its founding by Muhammad in the seventh century, the Islamic religion spread rapidly. By the eighth century, it dominated lands stretching from Spain to India. After Muhammad's death, a split over the question of succession to the Islamic leadership created two main branches, or sects, of Islam—the Shiites and the Sunnis.

The **inside of a Persian mosque.** While the architecture of a mosque is usually simple, the surface decorations are elaborate, featuring intricate calligraphy, delicate floral designs, and complex geometric patterns. Visit vgsbooks.com to learn more about Islam.

Nearly 90 percent of Iranians belong to the Shiite sect of the Islamic religion, and about 10 percent follow the Sunni sect. Whatever their branch, all Muslims support the five pillars of Islam—profession of the faith, fasting during the holy month of Ramadan, donations to the poor, daily prayer, and a pilgrimage to Mecca, the site of Muhammad's birth.

In general, the Islamic government in Iran does not tolerate minority faiths, but some, including Judaism and Christianity, continue to exist. Zoroastrianism, the state religion of pre-Islamic Persia, is still practiced by a small Iranian minority. Most Zoroastrians live in Yazd, Shiraz, Kerman, Tehran, and Esfahan. Zoroastrianism, which started about 550 B.C. with Zoroaster, was one of the first religions to teach the idea of one supreme god.

Iran is also connected with Bahaism, a faith that originated in Persia in the 1840s. Bahais believe in the unity of all the important world religious leaders—Muhammad, Jesus, Gautama Buddha, Hindu Krishna, Zoroaster, and the Judaic prophets. Ayatollah Khomeini's regime forbade the Bahai to practice their religion. Officially, no Bahais are left in Iran, although it is estimated that more than 300,000 Bahais still reside there.

Social Customs and the Role of Women

In Iran the honor and unity of the family are more important than all other social bonds. A father or husband is head of the clan and has great influence and power in all decisions that affect the family. One's place in the family underlies Iran's social structure. Males have more formal authority than females, and young people are expected to respect and obey their elders.

Since inheritance is passed through men, they are the principal property holders and generally choose marriage partners for the unmarried women of their families. Often people who are related to one another will live in their own section of a village, and cousins may marry each other under Islamic law.

ZOROASTRIANISM

Until the Arab conquest in the seventh century, Persians practiced Zoroastrianism. The religion was founded by Zoroaster in the sixth century B.C. It was one of the first religions to believe in an all-seeing, invisible god, called Ahura Mazda. Zoroaster also preached the idea of the eternal struggle between good and evil. These two opposing forces were present in the supreme being and in all living things.

YOUNG PEOPLE

Because unrelated men and women are not allowed to mingle together, young people have a hard time meeting members of the opposite sex. In fact, a ban exists on public dating, and boys and girls may not openly socialize. Young people in social settings that involve boys and girls together are usually chaperoned by older family members. Punishments for those who disobey these rules include arrest and flogging. Because of such restrictions, Iranian marriages are often arranged by parents.

Iranian society is segregated by gender, meaning women and men are often separated. For example, men and women sit in separate sections on city buses, go to different schools, and stand in different lines at the markets. In 1999 the Iranian legislature passed a law that forbade women from going to male doctors. Men visit male doctors, while women must see female doctors.

Under Iran's Islamic government, women hold a less visible position in society than they did before the revolution. Women are encouraged to practice *hejab*, or modest dress. Many women cover themselves with the *chador*, a head-to-foot garment including a veil that hides them from public view. Some women

Iranian men and women stand in **separate lines** to board buses and other public transportation. Men and women also sit separately.

This female photographer is **wearing a chador while working.** Iranian women are expected to cover themselves whenever they leave their homes.

choose to wear a less traditional covering called a manteau, which is more like an overcoat.

Nevertheless, Iran's religious regime has not denied women the right to vote, and about 4 percent of the Majlis is female. In addition, Iranian women can go to college, and many women work outside the home in administrative positions and in other professions. Women who are part of some nomadic tribes often have even higher status and may mingle freely with men.

Education

Iranian law requires that all children between the ages of six and ten attend school. Some remote rural areas, however, do not have schools. Nevertheless, about 95 percent of Iran's children receive at least a primary education. Most primary and secondary schools are state operated, and all schools fall under the authority of the Ministry of Education and Training. Elementary and university education is free, and small fees are charged for state-run secondary schools. Textbooks are issued free to children in the primary grades.

Secondary education starts at age eleven and consists of three years of middle school and four years of high school. Students in high school may choose from several different programs, including general academics, vocational or technical training, and science and math. All students must learn the Quran, regardless of their field of study.

Iranian boys may choose to attend a **Quranic, or religious, school.** Recently, religious schools have gained prominence over nonreligious schools.

Iran has about two hundred universities and colleges. After the 1979 revolution, the government closed all of Iran's higher education institutions until they had eliminated all Western teachings from their courses and were focused only on Islamic ideals. Higher education is also free, but university students must work in the government for the number of years equal to the time they spend at the university.

Adult literacy had risen to 73 percent by 1997, although men are usually better educated than women. More than 85 percent of all Iranian men are literate, and about 70 percent of Iranian women can read and write. Women are allowed to go to school, but boys and girls are educated separately.

Religious education has taken precedence over nonreligious education, and funding for secular (nonreligious) programs has been greatly reduced. The enrollment at Islamic schools of higher education in Qom, the center of Islamic studies, is growing at a fast pace.

Health

After the Islamic Revolution in 1979, many Western-trained doctors and nurses fled from Iran. This shortage of trained medical professionals led to a decline in health care during the 1980s. Small villages and remote areas suffered the most. While conditions improved in the 1990s, shortages of medical personnel and supplies, especially in rural areas, continue to be a problem.

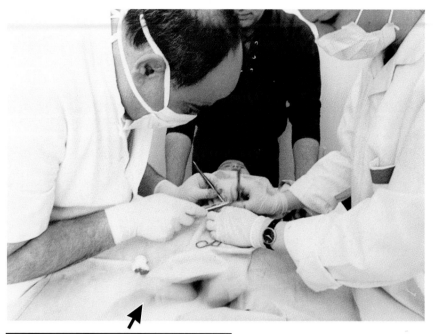

Iranian doctors operate on an infant. Iran's health care system, while improving, still suffers from shortages of doctors and medical supplies.

According to the 1979 constitution, the Iranian government is obligated to provide each citizen with insurance. The government established several programs to aid people who are ill or unable to work. Pensions are available for older people and for those families whose members are wounded or killed in war.

Iran's birthrate of 18 new infants for each 1,000 people is low compared to the region's average of 26. The infant mortality rate—32 deaths per 1,000 live births—is low for southern Central Asia, which averages about 69, but is still far above U.S. and European averages of 7 and 8, respectively. The eradication of smallpox and bubonic plague and the near elimination of malaria and cholera have helped extend life expectancy, which is 69 years for both men and women.

A population boom in the 1970s and 1980s threatened to limit the government's ability to provide adequate food supplies and health care. To combat this, the government instituted a national family planning program in the 1990s to slow down Iran's population growth. A national campaign encouraged families to have no more than two children. Family planning efforts, such as establishing programs and making contraceptives widely available, have contributed to this decline. As a result, the projected population for 2025 is 84.7 million, reflecting a growth of 1.2 percent. The government continues to work to slow this rate.

CULTURAL LIFE

Iran's rich cultural life reflects the Persian and Islamic influences that shaped the ancient as well as the modern nation. Many important Iranian art forms—such as poetry, pottery, and textiles—actually predate the Islamic conquest. But because Islam plays a pivotal role in Iranian daily life, it is rare to find artwork completely empty of religious undertones.

Language and Literature

Persian (also called Farsi), the principal language of Iran, is of Indo-European origin. It is related to most languages of Europe and southern Asia. Among the other Middle Eastern languages spoken in the country are Kurdish, various forms of Turkish, and Arabic.

Persian is very old, dating back to the seventh century B.C. Some ancient Persian documents survive, the most important of which are from the Sassanian period. Persian is second only to Arabic as the language of Islam, and for a long time, it was an important

means of spreading culture and literature to a region stretching from China to Turkey. Persian is still spoken in Iran, Afghanistan, and parts of Turkey.

Poetry is the oldest and most important literary form in Iran. While several works composed in the ninth century A.D. have been discovered, most Iranians consider Abdul Zasim Firdawsi their first great poet. Firdawsi, who lived from 940 to 1020, wrote *Shaname*, meaning "Book of Kings," Iran's national epic. *Shaname* recounts the trials and accomplishments of four dynasties of ancient Persian rulers.

The city of Shiraz is associated with the greatest Persian literature. It was the home of two of the country's best-loved poets—Sadi and Hafez—who lived in the thirteenth and fourteenth centuries, respectively. Sadi's masterpiece, *Golestan (The Rose Garden)*, combines prose and poetry. In addition to penning about seven hundred love poems, Hafez wrote the *Divan*, which many modern Iranians still quote.

A statue of Omar Khayyam. While Omar Khayyam was an important Persian mathematician, he is best remembered as the author of the *Rubaiyat.*

Of all the Persian poets, however, most familiar worldwide is Omar Khayyam. An eleventh-century mathematician, astronomer, and poet, Omar Khayyam is best known as the author of the *Rubaiyat,* a collection of rhyming verses.

Contemporary poets include Behar and Iraz Mirza. One of the rare female poets was Parvin Etesami, who was famous for her religious poems, "Mecca of the Heart" and "Eye and Heart." In addition to poetry, modern Iranian writers have adopted the novel format. Probably the most famous Iranian novelist outside of Iran is Sadeq Heydat, a contemporary author who penned *Buf I kur (The Blind Owl).* One of the few female writers is Simin Daneshvar, whose novel *Shaveshun* examines life in Iran between the two world wars.

◉ Arts and Crafts

Carpet making is the best known Iranian art form. The origins of Persian rug making date back as early as the fifth century B.C. Most of these early patterns consisted of complex geometric and floral designs. By the seventh century A.D., Persian carpets were exported to kingdoms as far away as China. After the Arab conquest, carpet weavers began adding Quranic verses to their designs. The reign of Shah Abbas I (1587–1629) is typically considered the pinnacle of Persian carpet production.

Modern Iranian weavers continue to produce high-quality carpets with intricate designs. The worldwide fame of Persian rugs is due to the delicacy of their knotting, the novelty of their designs, and the durability of their colors. Different regions develop patterns that use distinctive motifs and special dyes. Most carpets are made of either silk or wool. While some factories use machines to produce their carpets, many weavers continue to weave their wares by hand.

Islam forbids representational art, meaning humans (and animals among strict followers of Islam) are not depicted in true-to-life forms. Instead, geometric shapes and floral patterns decorate buildings and other art forms. Another important decorative element is calligraphy, an elaborate form of writing. Artists who copy the Quran in ornate fashion are highly regarded, and they have created a number of calligraphic styles. Shiraz and Esfahan became centers for calligraphy in the sixteenth century, producing some of the best calligraphy in the Muslim world.

One of the best-known forms of Iranian art is the miniature, a painting of great detail on a very small scale. This art form, developed in the fifteenth century, was exported to other cultures and sometimes was used to keep historical records of early civilizations. Favorite subjects include hunting and sports scenes.

An Iranian weaver uses a handloom to create the complex designs that have made Persian rugs famous.

Other popular crafts include pottery, one of the oldest Persian art forms. Colorful and detailed ceramics and tiles remain an important ware in many Iranian markets. Metalwork—in the form of plates, vases, and trays—is popular in Shiraz and Kerman, where artists use copper and other metals for cutting and engraving. Leatherwork is highly regarded and is used to decorate book bindings and handbags. Special woodwork, known as marquetry, is also important. Crafters create designs by inserting pieces of shells or metals into several different types of wood, especially walnut, betel, and cypress. Designs are usually religious. Then the woodwork is varnished. This art form is used for furniture and decorative boxes.

Architecture

Persian architecture is world famous, and many consider Iranian mosque design one of the country's biggest contributions to world culture. Since the emergence of Islam in Iran, Persian architecture has been a driving force for architecture in other Islamic countries.

A distinctive feature of Persian architecture is the use of a simple structure with lavish surface decoration. Most Persian buildings, which are often religious in nature, feature a courtyard and arcades, a domed roof, grand entrances, and four *iwans* (vaulted halls that open onto the courtyard). Islamic touches include high pointed arches and minarets (tall towers from which criers summon Muslims to prayer).

The **interior square of Jameh (Friday) Mosque** in Esfahan. The mosque features a combination of several different Persian architecture styles. Each dynasty added new elements to the mosque without destroying the others. Find links to more photos of Iranian architecture at vgsbooks.com.

While a building's structure may be simple in design, the surfaces are lavishly adorned with bright colors and intricate, complex details. This creates the illusion of the buildings being more complex than they really are. Because Islam forbids the depiction of living beings, Persian architects incorporated geometric designs, floral patterns, and calligraphic writing to decorate the surface area. Walls, floors, towers, and domes may all be covered in ceramic tiles laid out in intricate patterns, often arranged to form verses from the Quran. Important examples of Persian architecture include the Jameh Mosque in Esfahan, from the Seljuk period; the Kabud Mosque in Tabriz, the best surviving example from the Timurid dynasty; and the Golestan Palace in Tehran, from the elaborate Qajar style.

Theater and Film

Iranian theater predates the Arab conquest, but most modern forms of theater in Iran are based on Islam. The most important type of play is the *taziyeh*, or passion play, which takes place in every Iranian city and village on the anniversary of the death of Imam Hossein, Muhammad's grandson. Actors reenact the battle and murder of Hossein. Musicians play instruments—including flutes and drums—as performers read or sing traditional poems and songs.

Iranian film billboard

Filmmaking has been a popular art form since the opening of *The Lur Girl*, filmed in 1933. While action films are a popular genre for filmmakers, Iranian realistic cinema has only recently gained a wide audience. These films focus on daily life in Iran, often through the eyes of its children, and have become popular abroad.

Iranian films, like all of its other art forms, must comply with Islamic restrictions. Men and women do not touch on screen, and certain subjects such as suicide and adultery are not allowed. Some directors have drawn criticism from conservatives for pushing these boundaries. Among these directors is Abbas Kiarostami, whose *Taste of Cherry* was restricted in Iran because it dealt with suicide. Director Marzieh Meshkini's *The Day I Became a Woman*, a collection of three short films depicting women's lives in Iran, was also restricted. Important Iranian films include *Blackboards*, *The White Balloon*, and *A Time for Drunken Horses*, which won three awards at the Cannes Film Festival in 2000. The Iranian government banned all three films.

A dervish musician strums a *tanboor*, a three-stringed instrument dating back to 1500 B.C. The tanboor is the leading instrument played in dervish spiritual ceremonies.

Music

After the Islamic Revolution in 1979, the Ayatollah Khomeini banned popular Persian music and all Western music, including classical composers such as Mozart. Persian poetry accompanied by traditional Iranian instruments was the only musical form allowed.

In the late 1980s and throughout the 1990s, the government eased its restrictions on music, although Western music is still officially forbidden. Most Iranians, however, are familiar with Western pop music due to contraband tapes, TV, and the Internet.

Iran has its own rich musical heritage. Classical music is poetry accompanied by traditional musical instruments, including the stringed *tar*; drums like the *dahol* and *zarb*; the *nay* and *sorna*, a flute and oboe; and a tambourine called a *daryereh*. Shahram Nazeri is one modern musician who specializes in Iranian classical music.

Folk music remains popular among minority groups and mountain groups. This type of music varies from region to region, but the lyrics usually revolve around Islam. Traditional instruments and melodies characterize most Iranian folk music.

Iranian pop music also revolves around Islam. Some singers are slowly pushing the boundaries of the government's restriction, however. Some songs even borrow rhythms from Western dance music. Popular Iranian singers include Shadmehr Aghili, who sings mostly love songs, and the female star Googosh, who was popular in Iran before the Islamic Revolution and who has recently received permission to perform again.

Holidays and Festivals

Most Iranian holidays revolve around Islam. Religious holidays are frequently celebrated with a public holiday as well. The most important religious holiday is Ramadan, the month of fasting. During Ramadan, people do not eat after sunrise or before sunset. This extensive fasting is to remind the faithful of their dependence on Allah (God) and to cleanse their bodies. A three-day festival known as Eid-al Fetr marks the end of Ramadan. Muslims pour into the streets to celebrate, and everyone feasts. Other religious holidays include the birthday of the prophet Muhammad and the birthdays of famous imams (spiritual leaders).

One of the most important Iranian holidays, No Ruz, is not religious. No Ruz celebrates the Persian New Year. The twelve-day festival occurs in the spring, around March 21, and includes lighting small bonfires to symbolize the sun. People then jump over them to burn away bad luck. Families also gather for a special feast. Many families travel to the countryside on the last day of No Ruz for a picnic.

Public holidays include Oil Nationalization Day on March 20, Islamic Republic Day on April 1, and Revolution Day on June 5. Important festivals include the Fajir International Film Festival in February and the Tehran and Iranian Epic Music Festival in April.

Food and Clothing

Rice and kebabs (grilled meat and vegetables) are staple foods of Iran, and the national drink is tea. Rice spiced with Indian mango (a tropical fruit) is often served with an egg broken over it or with herbs, such as saffron, and bits of mutton (lamb). Iranians usually eat bread with their meals.

A typical dinner may consist of a thick soup, rice, vegetables, and yogurt. A popular local dish consists of chunks of mutton covered with a syrupy sauce made with pomegranate juice. Vegetable leaves stuffed with rice, as well as skewered meat or fish cooked over a grill, are also favorites in Iran. Iranians are fond of sweet flavors—such as honey and glazed fruits—and they sometimes sip tea through a sugar cube clenched in the jaw.

TAR HALVAH

Halvah is a confection that probably originated in the eastern Mediterranean region. The ingredients are combined and heated, then formed into bars or long loaves. Many Iranians break their Ramadan fast with a cup of tea and a piece of tar halvah.

1 lb. unsalted butter

3 c. flour

2 c. water

1¾ c. sugar

2 tbsp. rosewater

1 tsp. saffron dissolved in 1 tbsp. hot water

1. Over medium heat, melt butter in saucepan. Stir in flour one quarter cup at a time. Cook for 15 to 20 minutes, or until flour is golden brown. Remove from heat and set aside.
2. In a small saucepan, combine water and sugar. Bring to boil and reduce heat. Simmer for 5 minutes. Stir in rosewater and saffron.
3. Drizzle syrup mixture into the flour mixture, stirring constantly. Continue to stir until mixture thickens.
4. Pour halvah onto serving platter. Smooth the surface, and allow the mixture to cool for half an hour.

Makes 20 to 30 pieces.

After the Islamic Revolution, the Iranian government instituted a mandatory code of dress called hejab (meaning modest Islamic dress). Men are expected to dress conservatively, in long pants and long-sleeved shirts, even in the hottest summer months. Women must cover their entire bodies, except for their hands and faces. According to Islamic law, it is very important that women cover their hair in public. Many women have adopted the chador, a full-length covering that is often black. People who live in urban areas sometimes wear European-style clothing, including T-shirts. Some men dress in the long, flowing robes and turbans that form part of traditional Islamic dress.

In rural regions, men may wear roughly woven shirts and baggy trousers. Sometimes an outer garment is also worn. Village women often dress in clothing that fits their daily tasks, which usually revolve around farming or herding. They wear loose blouses and trousers and cover their heads with scarves.

◉ ▶ Sports and Recreation

Sports in Iran are gender segregated, meaning that public attendance is usually limited to men. Women's sports facilities are rare. Despite government reservations, soccer is the most popular sport in Iran. The national team qualified for the 1998 World Cup, and several Iranian athletes play in European leagues.

Wrestling remains the second most popular sport, and Iranian wrestlers often compete in international competitions. Other common sports include volleyball, basketball, horse riding, polo, and cricket, which is similar to baseball.

Teahouses are popular spots for Iranians, where regulars sip cup after cup of tea while they visit. Another unique recreational activity is Quranic recital contests. A variety of contestants, ranging from elderly men to young boys, demonstrate their powers of memorization at these events. Many urban homes also have television sets, although most people prefer to spend their leisure time visiting relatives and friends.

Wrestling has always been a popular sport in Iran. Some wrestlers train at a gym called a *zurkhaneh*, meaning "house of power." In modern zurkhanehs, ten to fifteen men demonstrate their strength with ritualized dances and demonstrations. Drums and poetry recitations usually accompany these performances.

Teahouse and **wrestling gymnasium.** Many Iranians like to gather with friends at teahouses. Some Iranian wrestlers train in a zurkhaneh—a special gym featuring an eight-sided pit where the athletes practice.

THE ECONOMY

Iran's economy revolves around three sectors—public, cooperative, and private. The public sector, which is run by the state, consists of large industries involving trade, banking, mining, insurance, energy and irrigation, transportation, and communications. The cooperative sector includes production and distribution of food, and the private group is made up of small-scale farmers and urban merchants who own their own businesses.

Iran's economy relied on its substantial oil reserves for most of the twentieth century. Despite having the world's fifth largest oil reserves, Iran has an unstable economy. The 1979 revolution resulted in the loss of thousands of workers as people opposed to the new government fled. This meant that industries lost managers, technicians, and many trained workers. Facing a shortage of skilled workers and resources, factories and businesses shut down. In addition, international conflict, including war with Iraq, and a global slowdown in the oil market had forced Iran deep into debt by the early 1990s.

The government is working to diversify Iran's oil-reliant economy by encouraging the development of new industries and resources. But the country lacks the resources and funds necessary to make these changes alone. Some politicians believe that foreign investment is essential to achieve this goal, but many conservatives argue that foreign investment is unconstitutional and against Quranic law. Whether or not these reforms succeed in stabilizing the country's economy, oil will remain Iran's lifeblood for many years to come.

○ Oil and Mining

Mining makes up 9 percent of Iran's gross domestic product (GDP, the total value of goods and services produced by a country in a year). Oil and natural gas dominate this sector, contributing 8 percent of the GDP at the beginning of the twenty-first century. While mining remains an important source of revenue, it employs less than 1 percent of the country's workforce.

Oil is by far the most important mining product for Iran. Oil was first discovered in Iran in 1908. The country's main oil fields are located in the Khuzestan Plain. At the beginning of the twenty-first century, Iran's oil reserves were estimated at 130,000 million barrels, after the discovery of a new deposit in the Azadegan oil field in the southwest. This discovery, added to known reserves, potentially makes Iran the largest producer of oil in the Middle East. Petroleum has also been discovered in Qom, in the central desert areas, and under the waters of the Persian Gulf.

After the revolution in 1979, the government nationalized oil companies, meaning that the state took control of the industry. The National Iranian Oil Company explores for new oil deposits, extracts the oil, and operates all aspects of refining and distribution.

Iran contains the world's second largest reserves of natural gas. Natural gas is found in the Elburz Mountains and in Khorasan Province. Pipelines serve the cities of Tehran, Kashan, Esfahan, Shiraz, Mashhad, and Ahvaz.

A wide variety of mineral deposits exist in addition to oil and natural gas. Coal is mined in fairly large quantities near Tehran, and workers extract iron ore from sites near Arak and in southern Kerman Province. Other important metals and metal ores include manganese, zinc, copper, lead, and chromium. Iran mines valuable deposits of rock salt, sulfates, and other raw materials for chemical production.

Quarries that produce stone for building and gypsum (used in making plaster) exist on a large scale. Alabaster and marble are found in lesser quantities. Gemstones include emeralds and topazes, and carnelians and turquoises are important semiprecious stones.

⏵ Industry

When the shah began his modernization programs in 1963, Iran's new production projects encouraged foreign investment to expand the country's underdeveloped industry. Esfahan built the largest textile mill in Iran, as well as a large sugar mill, a cement factory, and a huge steel mill. In Tehran, where workers once built buses by hand, a new plant began to mass-produce Iran's cars. The government continues to develop such industries to make the country less dependent on petroleum products.

Manufacturing makes up about 17 percent of Iran's GDP and employs almost 18 percent of the labor force. Iran's most important manufacturing sectors, outside of the oil industry, process foods, make textiles, and produce transportation equipment. Factories also turn out

furniture, machine tools, firearms, sugar, tea, soft drinks, caviar, leather footwear, and petroleum products. The country's steel industry is the largest in the Middle East.

Mass-production methods, however, have not been applied to the making of silks, carpets, and rugs. To preserve this national heritage, artisans still weave these products by hand on simple looms. The most popular carpets come from the cities of Tabriz, Kerman, Arak, Kashan, Esfahan, Shiraz, and Hamadan. In recent years, Tehran has also begun to turn out cotton fabrics.

Agriculture and Fishing

Because of its limited water supply, only about one-fourth of Iran's total land area can be farmed. Much of the country's food is imported. Yet agriculture, including forestry and fishing contributed about 21 percent of Iran's GDP. About 23 percent of the country's workforce is employed in agriculture.

SILK

Silk making is a long and involved process. Weavers often raise their own silkworms. Because the silkworms eat mulberry leaves, weavers must also grow and tend mulberry trees. Once the silkworms spin a silk cocoon around themselves, the weavers have just ten days before the worm transforms into a moth and destroys its silk cocoon. The weavers drop the cocoons into boiling water, killing the worm, and then unroll the silk. After they have the silk strands, weavers spin and dye the threads. These threads can then be woven into bolts of cloth.

Farmers walk past a field of sunflowers carrying bundles of goods. In rural areas, women help in the fields.

Most of Iran's farmers grow wheat, barley, and rice. In addition to these main crops, farmers cultivate cotton, tobacco, sugar beets, dates, olives, corn, tea, and citrus fruits. Pistachios and almonds are also grown for export.

Many nomadic tribes and small farming villages raise livestock, including herds of sheep, goats, and cattle. Horses, camels, donkeys, and water buffalo work as beasts of burden and produce meat and milk. The most important animal products, however, are wool for carpets and textiles and hides for leather.

Forests cover about 11 percent of the land, mostly near the Caspian Sea, and provide fuel and timber. Centuries of overcutting, however, have depleted the country's wooded areas. The state operates the timber industry, using most harvested wood for building. Iran's hardwoods include oak, beech, maple, Siberian elm, and walnut. Regions near the Zagros Mountains and in the provinces of Khorasan and Fars abound with pistachio, oak, maple, and walnut.

Fishing is a small but important industry, mostly concentrated along the Caspian Sea. Sturgeon, bream, whitefish, salmon, mullet, carp, catfish, and perch are common catches. Shrimp, sole, and tuna come from the Persian Gulf. Fishing is important both as a domestic

Iranian caviar, or fish eggs. Caviar from Iran's southern coastline of the Caspian Sea is considered some of the best in the world.

food source and as an export commodity. One of the most important fishing products is caviar. This salty delicacy is made from the eggs of sturgeon, and some varieties of Iranian caviar sell at high prices on the international market.

Heroin and Opium

A struggling economy and a rise in unemployment have contributed to several social problems, including drug smuggling and drug abuse. Heroin and opium are the leading narcotics in Iran, both in terms of profit and personal use.

After the 1979 revolution, Iran virtually eliminated the large-scale farming of opium poppies, but a few farmers continue to grow them. In their rough form, the poppies are used as opium. After refinement, the poppies become heroin. Both drugs may be smoked, eaten, or injected into the bloodstream and are highly addictive. Use of the drugs can lead to malnutrition, breathing problems, low blood pressure, and death.

The Iranian government continues to wage antidrug campaigns by enacting tougher laws for producing and smuggling the drugs. Smugglers may be put to death if they are caught with a large quantity of either narcotic. By the twenty-first century, drug-related crimes accounted for 48 percent of Iran's prison population.

For many people, however, years of severe drought has left drug smuggling as the only viable livelihood. While the cultivation of poppies has been eradicated, Iran remains an important route from producers—many of whom are located in neighboring Afghanistan—to European consumers. In addition, producers find users within Iran to support the drug industry.

Iranian antidrug forces seized more than 250 tons (227 metric tons) of narcotics in 2000, although officials estimate that this amount represents only about 10 to 20 percent of all drugs smuggled across the country from Afghanistan. While Afghanistan's heroin industry took a hit in 2000, when its administration banned poppy growing, an unstable Afghan government may hamper Iran's efforts to stop drug trafficking.

Transportation and Communication

Iran's rugged terrain makes it expensive to modernize the country's transportation system. While Reza Pahlavi worked to improve transportation, only about half of the country's 102,976 miles (165,724 km) roadways were paved. Tehran is the hub of a system of roads that connects the city to the provincial capitals in Iran. Two paved highways run across the country from Turkey to Afghanistan and from Iraq to Pakistan.

HAVE A SEAT

On Iranian city buses, men and women, even if they are related, must sit separately. On bus trips between cities, families may sit together, but unrelated men and women still do not sit next to each other. In shared taxis, men may jump in and out of the back seat and front seat to avoid sitting next to unrelated women as more people enter the vehicle.

Few people own their own vehicles, due to expense and the lack of developed roads. Many Iranians travel in buses, which are modern and comfortable in urban areas. Animals and bicycles are also common forms of transportation in rural areas. Ferries take passengers across Lake Urmia and to ports on the Caspian seacoast.

Iran has about 4,039 miles (6,500 km) of railroads. The major line runs from the Caspian Sea through Tehran to the Persian Gulf. Other important lines link Tehran to the cities of Khorramshahr, Gorgan, and Mashhad. An intercontinental line connecting Europe and Turkey through Iran is under construction. The Tehran Urban and Suburban Railway Company is constructing an underground railway to operate in Tehran and its suburb of Karaj.

Buses are an important form of transportation in Iran's cities. The illustration on the side of this bus is reminding people to conserve water.

Iranian men pore over a variety of newspapers at a newsstand. While many Iranians are well read, newspapers and other media are subject to government censorship.

Iran Air is the state-owned airline. There are seven international airports, including terminals at Bandar Abbas, Esfahan, Mashhad, Shiraz, Tabriz, Tehran, and Zahedan. In addition, Iran's government is working to construct several new terminals and to improve existing airports.

Principal shipping ports on the Persian Gulf include Khark Island for oil and Bandar-e Shahid Rajai, Bandar-e Khomeini, Bushehr, Bandar Abbas, and Chah Bahar for commercial ports. Khorramshahr, Iran's largest shipping port, was almost completely destroyed during the war with Iraq. The government is working to rebuild it. In the meantime, other principal ports include Bandar-e Anzali and Bandar-e Nowshahr on the Caspian Sea.

Radio is the most important form of communication in Iran, although some households own television sets. Television and radio operate under the National Iranian Radio and Television Organization. All broadcasts and newspapers are strictly censored by the government. It is illegal to publish anything critical of Islam.

Modern Iranian businesses often use **computers** in their daily operations, yet few individuals own computers at home.

While a portion of the population also owns telephones and computers, these forms of communication continue to be relatively limited.

The Future

Iran's future remains largely uncertain. To become economically stable, the government must develop financial sectors that do not rely on oil. While President Khatami recognizes the country's need for a diversified economic base, the conservative Islamic government is reluctant to allow foreign investment into the country.

Iran also faces several obstacles on the international scene. Iran has not resolved long-standing conflicts with many of its Muslim neighbors, particularly Iraq. Despite attempts to reconcile relations with the United States and many European countries, Iran has yet to establish strong diplomatic links with these countries.

 Visit vgsbooks.com, where you will find links to up-to-date information about Iran's economy and a converter where you can find the most current exchange rate and change U.S. dollars to Iranian rial.

Internal unrest also plagues the country's future. The unstable economy and conservative political system have led to dissatisfaction among the general populace. Some minority groups, such as the Kurds, have openly rebelled. And the government's restrictions on women have garnered criticism both at home and abroad. In addition, social problems such as drug smuggling and drug abuse present new challenges for Iran's people.

If Iran is able to overcome its economic problems and to find a politically stable place in the international community, a better future may yet be possible for this strong Islamic nation. Balancing its Islamic goals with economic and social development will continue to challenge Iran in the coming decades.

IRAN AND THE UNITED STATES

Iran and the United States have been at odds since the mid-twentieth century, when the United States controlled part of the country's oil industry. To protect its interests, the U.S. government supplied aid to the shah's military and secret police. Many Iranians despised this foreign influence. During the Islamic Revolution, Khomeini called the United States "the Great Satan." Tensions worsened during the 1980s when the United States backed Iraq in the Iran-Iraq War. While Khatami has made limited attempts to reestablish diplomatic relations with the United States, both governments still regard each other with suspicion.

President Khatami addresses a crowd. Khatami and his reforms have drawn criticism from both conservative and liberal Iranians.

3000 B.C.	Elamites settle in the area of modern Iran.
1000 B.C.	Aryan peoples migrate to Iran from Central Asia.
553 B.C.	Cyrus the Great establishes an empire that stretches into Egypt, Greece, and Russia.
334–330 B.C.	Alexander the Great conquers Persia and makes it part of his Greek Empire.
A.D. 224	Ardashir founds the Sassanian dynasty.
600s	Arabs conquer the Sassanians and introduce the religion of Islam to the area.
900s	Firdawsi writes some of his most famous works, including *Shaname*.
1220	Mongol tribes begin invading Persia.
1380	Mongol ruler Timur the Lame establishes the Timurid dynasty in Iran.
1400s	The art of miniatures develops.
1500	Persia falls completely under Safavid rule.
1587	Safavid shah Abbas I ascends the throne and unifies the kingdom of Persia.
1722	Afghan invaders conquer the Safavids.
1727	Nader Qoli Shah defeats Afghan forces in Persia.
1794	Turkish Qajars seize power in Persia.
1840s	The Bahai religion is founded in Iran.
1906	The Majlis, or legislature, is established.
1908	British excavations discover oil in the Persian Gulf.
1914–1918	British and Russian troops occupy Persia during World War I.
1921	Reza Khan leads a coup against Qajar and British rule in Persia.
1926	Reza Khan establishes the Pahlavi dynasty and changes his name to Reza Shah Pahlavi.
1933	Iranian cinema begins with the making of the film *The Lur Girl*.
1935	The shah officially changes Persia's name to Iran.
1941	Reza Shah is forced to resign his throne.
1951	The Iranian government nationalizes the British-run oil industry.

1962 Shah Mohammed Reza Pahlavi redistributes land in a
      reform called the White Revolution and works to modernize the
      country according to Western influences.

1963 Iranian women receive the right to vote. Shah Pahlavi has the Ayatollah
      Khomeini, a religious leader and opponent of Pahlavi, arrested. Khomeini
      is imprisoned, leading to mass demonstrations by Khomeini supporters.

1964 The Ayatollah Khomeini is freed from prison and forced into exile.

1979 The shah flees Iran, and the Ayatollah Khomeini returns from exile. Iranians vote
      to found the Islamic Republic of Iran. Khomeini becomes wali faqih.

1980 Iraqi forces invade Khuzestan, starting an eight-year conflict with Iran.

1988 Iran and Iraq agree to a cease-fire.

1989 The Ayatollah Khomeini dies. Ayatollah Ali Khamenei succeeds him as wali faqih.

1997 Moderate Sayed Mohammad Khatami is elected president.

1998 The Iranian soccer team qualifies to compete in the World Cup.

1999 The legislature votes to limit freedom of the press. Demonstrations in Tehran lead to
      hundreds of arrests.

2000 The government is forced to impose water and electricity rations to combat shortages
      due to an extended drought.

2001 Khatami is reelected.

2002 Iran denies having any connection to the terrorist attack on the United States at the
      World Trade Center towers in New York City and at the Pentagon near Washington, D.C.,
      on September 11, 2001. President George W. Bush declares that Iran is part of the "axis
      of evil," along with Iraq and North Korea.

2003 Already strained relations between the United States and Iran are worsened by
      accusations from the Bush administration that Iran has an active nuclear weapons
      program. Prorefrom students in Iran increase demonstrations against the conser-
      vative Islamic government, demanding greater freedoms.

COUNTRY NAME Islamic Republic of Iran

AREA 636,296 square miles (1,648,007 sq. km)

MAIN LANDFORMS Caspian lowlands, Dasht-e-Kavir, Dasht-e-Lut, Elburz Mountains, Khuzestan Plain, Plateau of Iran, Zagros Mountains

HIGHEST POINT Mount Damavand, 18,934 feet (5,771 m) above sea level

LOWEST POINT sea level

MAJOR RIVERS Karun, Safid, Zayandeh

ANIMALS Asiatic cheetah, Baluchistan bear, fox, ibex, jackal, panther, Persian fallow deer, rabbit, tiger, wolves

CAPITAL CITY Tehran

OTHER MAJOR CITIES Mashhad, Esfahan, Tabriz, Shiraz

OFFICIAL LANGUAGE Farsi (Persian)

MONETARY UNIT Rial. 100 dinars = 1 rial; 10 rials = 1 touman.

IRANIAN CURRENCY

Iran's official monetary unit is the rial. Iran's currency, like the country itself, has gone through many changes in recent history. During the economic growth of the 1960s and 1970s, Iran's currency peaked, becoming one of the most stable units of currency in the world. After the Islamic Revolution and the economic collapse due to war and a global slowdown in oil markets, the value of the rial plummeted. Rials are available in coins of 1, 2, 5, 10, 20, 50, 100, and 250, and notes of 100, 200, 500, 1,000, 5,000, and 10,000. Coins are marked in Farsi only, but notes have one side printed in English. The Iranian rial is not traded outside of the country.

Iran's flag was adopted July 29, 1980. It consists of horizontal green, red, and white stripes, with a red emblem in the center. The colors are traditional. Green represents Islam, white symbolizes peace, and red stands for courage. The emblem consists of four crescents, which are meant to stand for the word *Allah*, and a sword. The five parts of the emblem also symbolize the five pillars of Islam. The emblem's shape looks similar to a tulip, a symbol of the young people who have died for Iran. Stylized Arabic writing adorns the edges of the white strip. The writing is actually twenty-two copies of the Islamic phrase *Allahu Akbar*, or "God is Great."

Iran's national anthem has also undergone several changes since the mid-twentieth century. Under the shah, the "Imperial Salute" was the national anthem. A year after the Islamic Revolution, the new republic adopted an anthem by Mohammed Beglari-Pour. This was replaced a decade later with Iran's current national anthem, "Ey Iran." The current anthem was written by Hassan Riahi and was adopted in 1990.

Ey Iran
Upwards on the horizon rises the Eastern Sun,
The sight of the true Religion.
Bahman—the brilliance of our Faith.
Your message, O Imam, of independence and freedom
Is imprinted on our souls.
O Martyrs! The time of your cries of pain rings in our ears.
Enduring, continuing, eternal,
The Islamic Republic of Iran.

For a link where you can listen to Iran's national anthem, "Ey Iran," go to vgsbooks.com.

Flag   National Anthem

SHADMEHR AGHILI (b. 1972) Shadmehr Aghili is an Iranian singer and songwriter who specializes in pop music. While most pop music is limited in Iran, Aghili is allowed to record because the government believes his music will keep young people from listening to Western music. Aghili has not been allowed to perform in concert, however, and his music was officially banned for more than a year because the government believed he was becoming too popular. His CDs include *Mosaafer* and *Dehaati.*

ALI DAEI (b. 1969) Ali Daei is an Iranian soccer player who made his national team debut in 1993. He played in the 1996 Asian Cup and moved to Germany in 1997. In 1999 he was named Asian Player of the Year. Daei was born in Ardabil, Iran.

PARVIN ETESAMI (1907–1940) Born in Tabriz, Parvin Etesami was probably the most famous female Iranian poet of the twentieth century. Her works featured modern social commentary using the classic Persian poetic style. Her first collection of poems was published in 1935, and her most famous works include the *Divan of Parvin E'tesami.*

LIDA FARIMAN (b. 1972) In 1996 Lida Fariman became the first Iranian woman to attend the Olympics since the Islamic Revolution in 1979. She competed in the air-rifle shooting event, one of the few Olympic events deemed acceptable for women, wearing hejab. She also carried the Iranian flag for the Olympic team during the opening ceremony.

MAHMUD FARSHCHIAN (b. 1929) Mahmud Farshchian is a prominent Iranian artist and painter who has received international fame for his works. His paintings utilize Persian and Islamic traditions and techniques. In 1995 Farshchian received Iran's first degree Medal of Art and Culture. In 2001 he was commissioned to design the new mausoleum of Imam Reza. He was born in Esfahan.

GOOGOSH (b. 1951) Googosh is Iran's most popular female singer. She started performing at the age of five. During her career, she released a dozen hit albums and appeared in more than twenty movies. Following the Islamic Revolution in 1979, she was banned from performing in public. In 2000 the Iranian government lifted its ban and allowed Googosh to travel abroad to appear in a movie. She also received permission to perform her music again.

NASROLLAH KASRAIAN (b. 1944) Nasrollah Kasraian is an Iranian photographer whose works have been published in international magazines such as *Life* and in books, including *Our Homeland Iran.* Born in Khoramabad, he attended the University of Tehran. His works document many of the unique populations living within the borders of Iran. In addition, he has had exhibitions in Iran, France, and the United States.

SAYED MOHAMMAD KHATAMI (b. 1943) Born in Ardakan, Iran, Sayed Mohammad Khatami studied at a religious school as a boy and went on to Esfahan University and the University of Tehran. He became the culture minister in Iran's first parliament in 1982. In 1997 he became the fifth elected president of the Islamic Republic of Iran. A moderate, Khatami has promised to make political and social reforms, as well as to reestablish diplomatic relations with the United States and Europe.

RUHOLLAH KHOMEINI (1902–1989) Ruhollah Khomeini was a politician and religious leader born in the town of Khomeini. He became a respected religious scholar and teacher in Qom. But he was arrested and exiled in 1963 for opposing the shah's political reforms. He soon became a symbol of opposition for the Iranian populace. Khomeini returned to Iran in 1979, after the Islamic Revolution, and he helped establish the Islamic government that has led the country since.

SAMIRA MAKHMALBAF (b. 1980) Samira Makhmalbaf is a film producer and director who has produced several internationally acclaimed movies. She began her film career in 1987 when she played in her father's movie *The Cyclist*. After studying cinema as a teenager, she directed the movie *The Apple* at the age of seventeen. In 1998, at the age of eighteen, she became the youngest director in the world to participate in the Cannes Film Festival. Her second feature film, *The Blackboard*, won the Special Jury Prize at Cannes in 2000. She was born in Tehran.

OMAR KHAYYAM (ca. 1047–1123) Omar Khayyam was born in Neyshabur, Iran, during the Persian Empire. He is probably the most famous Iranian poet, and his works include the *Rubaiyat*, a collection of poetry. In Iran he is more famous as a mathematician, a historian, and an astronomer. Some of his most important work in these areas focused on algebra.

BISOTUN This site near Bakhataran includes one of the most famous relief carvings in Iran, commissioned by Darius I. Sculptures and reliefs from throughout the country's history may also be seen here.

GOLESTAN (ROSE) PALACE The Rose Palace of Tehran served as the residence of the Qajar kings. In the twentieth century, the palace was used by the shahs for special ceremonies, such as coronations.

GOLESTAN NATIONAL PARK Opened in 1957, this park along Iraq's Caspian seacoast actually covers two very different climatic zones—forest and semiarid. The park also is home to some of the country's most interesting wildlife.

MASHHAD The city of Mashhad is Iran's holiest city because of its shrine to the eighth imam of the Shiite sect. Highlights here include the tomb of Imam Reza, a thirteenth-century mosque, and a Safavid mosque.

NATIONAL ARCHAEOLOGICAL MUSEUM This museum in Tehran features the country's most important artifacts from both pre-Islamic and Islamic periods. Highlights include Elamite vases and a statue of the Persian ruler Darius I.

PASARGADAE These ancient ruins were once the thriving first capital of Persia under Cyrus the Great. Ancient records indicate that Cyrus founded his capital on the site where he and his army defeated the Medes about 553 B.C.

PERSEPOLIS The most impressive archaeological site in Iran, Persepolis features ruins from Persia's ancient empire. Highlights here include the Gate of All Nations, Darius's palace, and the Hall of a Hundred Columns.

POL-E KHAJU This is Esfahan's most famous and most picturesque bridge. Built by Shah Abbas II in 1650, the bridge features two stories of decorated arches and rich stone steps.

SUSA This ancient city in Khuzestan was a capital of Persia during the Elamite and Achaemenid Empires. While little is left of the city, ruins of the acropolis and of Darius I's palace are on view.

TAQ-E BOSTAN This Sassanian site near Bakhtaran is a series of grottoes and carvings into the cliff face. The grottoes feature elaborate wall decorations and sculptures.

TOMBS OF SADI AND HAFEZ Two of Iran's most famous poets are honored with mausoleums surrounded by beautiful gardens at this site. The tombs are the most important monuments in Shiraz.

ayatollah: an Islamic religious leader

coup d'état: a sudden and decisive political action, with or without force, that usually results in a change of government

Islam: a religion based on the prophet Muhammad's teachings and founded in the seventh century A.D. The holy book of Islam is the Quran, which holds the five fundamental religious duties (or pillars) for its followers.

mosque: an Islamic place of worship

Muslim: a follower of Islam

protectorate: a protected region or country under the control or partial control of another protecting nation

Quran: the holy book of Islam. Muslims accept the writings in the Quran as revelations made to Muhammad by Allah through the angel Gabriel.

refugee: a person forced to flee his or her country due to political upheaval

Sharia: Islamic laws set forth in the Quran

Shiite: a member of one of the two major Islamic sects. Shiites believe that only direct descendants of Muhammad are legitimate Islamic rulers.

Sunni: a member of one of the two major Islamic sects. Sunnis believe that Muhammad's successors could be chosen from among his closest colleagues and not necessarily from his direct relations.

United Nations: organization of world nations established to maintain world peace through resolution of international conflicts and through finding solutions to the world's social, economic, cultural, and humanitarian problems

Glossary

Selected Bibliography

Bernard, Cheryl, and Zalmay Khalilzad. *The Government of God: Iran's Islamic Republic.* **New York: Columbia University Press, 1984.**
The authors focus on the events of the Islamic Revolution of 1979 and its aftermath.

Cartlidge, Cherese. *Iran.* **San Diego: Lucent Books, 2002.**
Cartlidge's work focuses on the people and history of the country, with a special chapter on the challenges Iran will face in years to come.

CountryWatch. **November 2002.**
Website: <http://www.countrywatch.com> (November 11, 2002).
CountryWatch includes information such as political history, economic conditions, environmental issues, and social customs in Iran.

Daniel, Elton. *The History of Iran.* **Westport, CT: Greenwood Press, 2001.**
This book offers a new look at Iran through its rich and complex history.

Europa Year World Book. **Vol. 1. London: Europa Publications, 2001.**
The article covering Iran includes recent events, vital statistics, and economic information.

Garry, Lyle. *Iran.* **Philadelphia: Chelsea House Publishers, 1999.**
This book looks at Iran's history, geography, economy, and culture.

Ghods, M. Reza. *Iran in the Twentieth Century: A Political History.* **Boulder, CO: Lynne Rienner Publishers, 1989.**
Ghods covers the history and political forces that shaped Iran's political system from 1905 to the Islamic Revolution.

Islamic Republic News Agency, **2002.**
Website: <http://www.irna.com> (November 12, 2002).
This on-line news agency features current events for Iran.

Omar Khayyam. "Rubaiyat." *Internet Classics Archive: The Rubaiyat,* **2000.**
Website: <http://classics.mit.edu/Khayyam/rubaiyat.html> (July 1, 2003).
This on-line resource offers Omar Khayyam's most famous work, the *Rubaiyat,* in its entirety.

Population Reference Bureau, **2002.**
Website: <http://www.prb.org> (November 12, 2002).
The bureau offers current population figures, vital statistics, land area, and more. Special articles cover the latest environmental and health issues that concern Iran.

Statesman's Yearbook. **London: Macmillan, 2001.**
This resource features information about the country's historical events, industry and trade, climate and topography, as well as suggestions for further reading.

The World Factbook, 2002.
Website: <http://www.cia.gov/cia/publications/factbook.html> **(June 2, 2002).**
This website features up-to-date information about the people, land, economy, and government of Iran. Transnational issues are also briefly covered.

World Gazetteer, 2002.
Website: <http://www.gazetteer.de> **(June 2, 2002).**
The *World Gazetteer* offers population information about cities, towns, and places for Iran, including their administrative divisions.

Yale, Pat. *Iran.* Oakland: Lonely Planet Publications, 2001.
This guidebook offers information about the sights and highlights of Iran.

Avi-Yonah, Michael. *Dig This!: How Archaeologists Uncover Our Past.* Minneapolis: Runestone Press, 1993.
This book describes the history of archaeology, methods of archaeological excavation, and ancient civilizations, including some of those in ancient Persia.

Baker, Patricia. *Iran.* Buckinghamshire, UK: Bradt Travel Guides, 2001.
This guidebook offers basic sights to see, as well as advice on cultural awareness, when visiting Iran.

Barth, Linda. *Mohammed Reza Pahlavi.* New York: Chelsea House Publishers, 2002.
Read about Iran's last shah and his contributions to modern Iran.

Geography Department. *Sold!: The Origins of Money and Trade.* Minneapolis: Runestone Press, 1993.
This book explores trade and money in the ancient world, including Persian mining and use of precious metals.

Gherman, Beverly. *Jimmy Carter.* Minneapolis: Lerner Publications Company, 2004.
This biography chronicles the life and presidency of Jimmy Carter, including his administration's relations with Iran and the Iran hostage crisis.

Gonan, Rivka. Charge!: *Weapons and Warfare in Ancient Times.* Minneapolis: Runestone Press, 1993.
This study of the ancient world describes the development and use of early weapons and means of protection, including those developed by the ancient Persians.

Gordon, Matthew. *Ayatollah Khomeini.* New York: Chelsea House, 1987.

This biography covers the life of the religious leader who overthrew Iran's political system in 1979 and established an Islamic government in its place.

Iranian Cultural and Information Center
Website: <http://www.persia.org>
Learn more about the history and culture of Iran.

Laird, Elizabeth. *Kiss the Dust.* New York: Dutton, 1992.
Thirteen-year-old Tara, a Kurdish girl living in Iraq, must flee her cozy home to a crowded Iranian prison camp during the Iran-Iraq War.

Napoli, Donna Jo. *Beast.* New York: Atheneum, 2000.
This interpretation of the classic tale of *Beauty and the Beast* takes place in ancient Persia. Young Prince Orasmyn tells the story of the curse that causes his transformation from a human to a lion. The young prince must learn how to survive as a beast while retaining his humanity.

Omar Khayyam. *The Rubaiyat of Omar Khayyam.* New York: Penguin Classics, 1998.
This translation of Omar Khayyam's poems includes illustrations.

Further Reading and Websites

Salam Iran
Website: <http:www.salamiran.org>
This website features cultural and economic information, as well as current events in Iran.

Spencer, William. *The United States and Iran.* Brookfield, CT: Twenty-first Century Books, 2000.
This book describes the history of the strained relations between Iran and the United States.

vgsbooks.com
Website: <http://www.vgsbooks.com>
Visit vgsbooks.com, the homepage of the Visual Geography Series®, which is updated regularly. You can get linked to all sorts of useful online information, including geographical, historical, demographic, cultural, and economic websites. The vgsbooks.com site is a great resource for late-breaking news and statistics.

Wagner, Heather Lehr. *Iran.* New York: Chelsea House Publications, 2002.
Wagner looks at the modern nation of Iran and its increasingly important role in the Middle East.

Woods, Michael, and Mary B. Woods. *Ancient Agriculture: From Foraging to Farming.* Minneapolis: Runestone Press, 2000.
This book examines various cultures from the Stone Age to A.D. 476, including cultures of the Middle East.

———. *Ancient Computing: From Counting to Calendars.* Minneapolis: Runestone Press, 2000.
The authors examine the methods of computation developed in various world civilizations, including those of the Middle East, from prehistoric times to the end of the Roman Empire.

———. *Ancient Machines: From Wedges to Waterwheels.* Minneapolis: Runestone Press, 2000.
This book investigates the invention of six machines in various ancient civilizations, including Persian civilizations, from the Stone Age to the fall of the Roman Empire.

———. *Ancient Warfare: From Clubs to Catapults.* Minneapolis: Runestone Press, 2000.
The Woodses present and study examples of ancient weapons and warfare in Europe and Asia. The study includes Greek ruler Alexander the Great's exploits in Persia.

Zeinert, Karen. *The Persian Empire.* New York: Benchmark Books, 1997.
Explore the ancient Persian Empire, including the Persian script, the empire's history, and its most famous leaders.

Index

Abbas I, 19, 24, 25, 48
Abbasid dynasty, 23–24
Achaemenid dynasty, 21
Afghanistan, 4, 8, 9, 19, 25, 26, 40, 61
Aghili, Shadmehr, 52
Alexander the Great, 22
animals, 15, 60, 68
Arabs, 23, 36, 38–39
architecture, 18–19, 50–51
arts, 24, 48–50
Azeri, 38

Bahaism, 41
Bazargan, Mehdi, 30
Behar, 48
Bush, George W., 7, 34

calendars, 53
calligraphy, 24, 49
carpet making, 24, 39, 48–49, 59
Caspian Sea, 8, 9, 10, 12, 13, 14, 15, 16, 23, 60, 62
caviar, 59, 61
censorship, 28, 51, 63
chador. See clothing
China, 24, 47, 48
clothing, 27, 39, 42–43, 54
communication, 63–64
criminal justice system, 35
Cyrus the Great, 21, 22

Daneshvar, Simin, 48
Darius I, 22
Darius III, 22
deforestation. See forests and forestry
drugs, 61, 65

economy, 7, 28, 29, 32, 33, 56–61, 64, 65
education, 43–44
environmental challenges, 15–18
Esfahan, 19, 24, 25, 38, 41, 49, 58, 59, 63, 68
Etesami, Parvin, 48
earthquakes, 9, 17, 19
ethnic groups, 36, 37–39

farming, 59–60
Farsi, 27, 36, 46, 68

festivals, 52–53
Firdawsi, Abdul Zasim, 47
fish and fishery, 15, 59, 60–61
food, 53–54
forests and forestry, 14, 16–17, 59, 60

Googosh, 52
Great Britain, 4, 25, 26–27, 28, 29
Greece, 4, 21, 22, 23
Gulf War, 33

Hafez, 47
health care, 29, 44–45
Heydat, Sadeq, 48
holidays, 52–53
human rights, 29, 33, 34

industry, 58–59
instruments, 52
Iran: anthem, 69; cities, 18–19, 36, 69; climate, 13–14; currency, 68; early history, 20–25; flag, 69; flora and fauna, 14–15, 17–18; geographical regions, 8–10, 68; government, 35; independence, 27–28; Islamic Republic establishment, 30–31; maps, 6, 11; population, 36, 45; timeline, 66–67. See also Persia
Iran-Iraq War, 7, 16, 31–32, 63, 65
Iraq, 7, 8, 14, 24, 29, 33, 61, 65
Islam, 5, 23, 40–41, 46, 49, 50–51, 52, 65, 69; See also Shiite Muslims and Sunni Muslims
Islamic law. See Sharia

Khamenei, Ayatollah Ali, 32, 35
Khan, Reza. See Pahlavi, Reza Shah
Khatami, Sayed Muhammad, 7, 33, 34, 64
Khomeini, Ayatollah Ruhollah, 5, 7, 29, 30, 32, 33, 41, 52, 65
Kiarostami, Abbas, 51
Koran. See Quran
Kurds, 36, 38, 39, 65

language, 27, 36, 46, 68
literacy, 29, 44

Majlis, 26, 28, 35, 43

Malik-Shah, 24
manufacturing, 58–59
Mashad, 19, 68
Medes, 13, 20, 21, 38
Meshkini, Marzieh, 51
mining, 57–58
Mirza, Iraz, 48
Mohammad, Karim Khan Zand
    (Karim Khan), 25
Mongol rule, 24
Mosaddeq, Mohammad, 28–29
mosques, 18, 19, 24, 25, 36, 37, 50
movies, 51, 53
Muhammad, 7, 23, 35, 40, 53
music, 51, 52, 53

Nader Qoli, 25
Nasir al-Din Shah, 26
Nazeri, Shahram, 52
nomadic people, 10, 37, 39, 43, 60

oil production, 7, 5, 9, 10, 16, 20, 26,
    28, 31, 39, 56–58
Omar Khayyam, 48
Organization of Petroleum Exporting
    Countries (OPEC), 29

Pahlavi, Mohammed Reza, 27,
    28–30, 31
Pahlavi, Reza Shah, 27, 61
Pakistan, 8, 9, 21, 61
Persia, 4, 13, 19, 20, 21–28, 41, 47
Persian Gulf, 8, 10, 12, 14, 16, 17,
    32, 39, 58, 62, 63
petroleum. See oil production
poetry, 47–48, 52

Qajar dynasty, 25–27, 51
qanats, 13
Qom, 29, 44, 58
Quran, 35, 40, 43, 48, 49, 51

Rafsanjani, Ali Akbar Hashemi, 7,
    32, 33
Ramadan, 52–53
recipe, 54
recreation, 55
Riahi, Hassan, 69
rugs. See carpet making
Russia, 4, 12, 19, 25–26, 27–28, 29

Sadi, 47
Safavid dynasty, 24–25
Sassanians, 4, 23, 46
Saudi Arabia, 23
SAVAK, 29, 30, 33
Seleucid dynasty, 23
Seljuk Empire, 24, 51
Sharia, 5, 30, 54
Shiite Muslims, 5, 7, 19, 23, 24, 29,
    30, 31, 38, 39, 40–41
Shiraz, 19, 21, 38, 41, 47, 49, 50, 59,
    63, 68
Soviet Union. See Russia
sports, 55
Sunni Muslims, 5, 7, 23, 31, 38–41

Tabriz, 19, 24, 59, 63, 68
Tehran, 13, 16, 18, 24, 27, 28, 29, 30,
    31, 32, 34, 38, 41, 58, 59, 61, 62,
    63, 68
Tehran Declaration, 27
terrorism, 7, 31, 33
theater, 51
Timur the Lame, 24
transportation, 61–63
Turkey, 4, 8, 9, 14, 22, 25, 36, 47, 61,
    62

United Nations, 28, 32, 33
United States, 27, 28, 29, 31, 32, 33,
    34, 64, 65

veils. See clothing

wali faqih, 35
water, 12–13, 34, 59
Western influence, 5, 26, 27, 28, 29,
    30, 44, 52
women, 27, 29, 30, 35, 39, 41–43, 44,
    54, 55, 59, 62, 65
World War I, 26
World War II, 27
writers, 48

Zagros Mountains, 9, 12, 13, 17, 38,
    58, 60
Zahedi, Fazlollah, 29
Zoroastrianism, 23, 41

Captions for photos appearing on cover and chapter openers:

Cover: The Xerxes Gate, or Gate of All Nations, at Persepolis once opened to the grand halls of the ancient Persian city. Constructed between 486 and 465 B.C. under Xerxes I, son of Darius the Great, the gate is adorned by two bull-like guards and inscriptions in several languages, reminding visitors to be kind to and respectful of each other.

pp. 4–5 This painting from the Safavid period adorns a wall of Bazar-e Vakil, or Regent's Bazaar, in Kerman. The painting depicts a Persian relaxing at a traditional teahouse.

pp. 8–9 Mountains rise up in the background of the landscape near the city of Mashhad in northeastern Iran.

pp. 20–21 An impressive stone griffin (a mythical creature with the head of an eagle and the body of a lion) continues to watch over the ancient ruins of Persepolis. Construction of the city, once the capital of Persia, began under Darius I (Darius the Great) between 518 and 516 B.C. Subsequent rulers continued adding to the city until it reached its height more than one hundred years later. Greek forces, led by Alexander the Great, conquered Persepolis in 330 B.C., burning much of the city to the ground.

pp. 36–37 Iranians crowd a busy bazaar in the city of Shiraz in southwestern Iran. Vendors at Iranian bazaars sell many goods, including food, clothing, jewelry, and metalworks.

pp. 46–47 Beautiful artwork and fine calligraphy embellish this Persian manuscript from about 1650. Traditional bookmaking, still popular in Iran, combines craft and artistry.

pp. 56–57 An Iranian refinery prepares crude oil, purifying it for production of gasoline and other oil-based products. The Iranian government took control of, or nationalized, the oil industry in 1951. Iranians celebrate Oil Nationalization Day on March 20 in recognition of this event.

Photo Acknowledgments
The images in this book are used with the permission of: © Brian Vikander, pp. 4–5, 8–9, 10, 18–19, 25 (right); Ron Bell/Digital Cartographics, pp. 6, 11; © Tor Eigeland, pp. 12, 13, 55 (right), 58–59, 60; © TRIP/TH-FOTO WERBUNG, p. 14; © David A. Northcott/CORBIS, p. 15 (left); © Moshe Shai/CORBIS, p. 15 (right); © Jacques Langevin/CORBIS SYGMA, pp. 16, 17; © Marcus Rose/Panos Pictures, pp. 20–21, 32, 63; © Araldo de Luca/CORBIS, pp. 22–23; © Hulton|Archive by Getty Images, p. 25 (left); © Art Resource, p. 26; © Bettmann/Corbis, pp. 27, 28, 30, 31; © AFP/CORBIS, pp. 34, 65; © TRIP/A. Gasson, pp. 36–37; © TRIP/M. Cerny, p. 38; © TRIP/Ibrahim, pp. 39 (left), 45, 52; © Hutchison Library/Christina Dodwell, p. 39 (right); © Trygve Bølstad/Panos Pictures, pp. 40, 48; © TRIP/M. Good, pp. 42, 55 (left), 62 © Hutchison Library/Leslie Woodheed, p. 43; © Hutchison Library,p. 44; © The Art Archive/Museum of Islamic Art Cairo/Dagli Orti, pp. 46–47; © TRIP/Eric Smith, p. 49; © TRIP/J. Sweeney, p. 50; © Hutchison Library/Isabella Tree, p. 51; © TRIP/J. Ellard, pp. 56–57; AP/Wide World Photos, p. 64; © Cory Langley, p. 68.

Cover photo: © TRIP/Eric Smith. Back cover photo: NASA